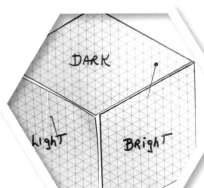

DARK

LIGHT   BRIGHT

with **25** **Quilts to Make**

Scrap Happy Quilts

from
Georgia Bonesteel

Schiffer
Publishing Ltd
4880 Lower Valley Road • Atglen, PA 19310

Other Schiffer Books on Related Subjects:

Southern Quilts: Celebrating Traditions, History, and Designs,
Mary W. Kerr, ISBN 978-0-7643-5502-8

Quilts in Everyday Life, 1855–1955: A 100-Year Photographic History,
Janet E. Finley, ISBN 978-0-7643-4216-5

Play-of-Color Quilting: 24 Designs to Inspire Freehand Color Play,
Bernadette Mayr, ISBN 978-0-7643-5533-2

Designed by Molly Shields
Type set in The BraggestDemo/Times New Roman
Quilt photography: Melissa Kilgore

ISBN: 978-0-7643-5632-2
Printed in China

Published by Schiffer Publishing, Ltd.
4880 Lower Valley Road
Atglen, PA 19310
Phone: (610) 593-1777; Fax: (610) 593-2002
E-mail: Info@schifferbooks.com
Web: www.schifferbooks.com

For our complete selection of fine books on this and related subjects,
please visit our website at www.schifferbooks.com. You may also write
for a free catalog.

Schiffer Publishing's titles are available at special discounts for
bulk purchases for sales promotions or premiums. Special editions,
including personalized covers, corporate imprints, and excerpts, can
be created in large quantities for special needs. For more information,
contact the publisher.

We are always looking for people to write books on new and
related subjects. If you have an idea for a book, please contact us at
proposals@schifferbooks.com.

*This book would not have been possible without the kind
assistance of graphic artist Samuel Baldwin, who created
the diagrams, patterns, and charts. —GB*

To all dedicated quilters

Age eighty is a proper amount of life
to ponder my path. What a surprise at
my birthday celebration to have all eight
grandchildren sing the following song,
written by my namesake, granddaughter
Georgia Elizabeth Smith.

Color Outside the Lines

Not everybody lives their life with a camera crew
Not everybody lives their life like you
Not everybody lives their life with people watching them doing their "thing"
Not everybody lives their life in the mountains with a rope swing.

But you taught us that it's always okay to color outside the lines
And you taught us that making art is what opens up your mind
And you taught us on your TV show a hundred different ways to quilt
And we have so many memories in this house you built.

There are a million different ways to tell a story
There are a million different ways to be heard
We know that it wasn't just for the glory
And that the quilts you made speak every word

From the plains of Iowa to sunny Florida to the Land of the Lakes, from Tulsa,
Oklahoma, to good old New Orleans, to the Blue Ridge mountains of home

You taught us it's always okay to color outside the lines
And you taught us that making art is what opens up your mind.
And you taught us on your TV show a thousand different ways to quilt
And we have so many memories in this house you built.

CONTENTS

A straight line is a line of duty and a curved line

is a line of beauty. —GB

INTRODUCTION

"I just can't stop making quilts."

Then I thought, "If I write a book, I'll have to stop, for awhile."

Certainly we have enough quilts here at Quilt Built. They pile up on beds, under beds, stacked in closets, neatly folded on shelves . . . they are thrown over chairs, rotated on walls and various quilt racks. That doesn't mean I haven't also considered the ceiling or even the floors. Once when filming a lap-quilting television show in the Netherlands at the Openlucht Museum, we discovered a quilt displayed under a thick, strong glass. We walked on the quilt. Ah, the possibilities are endless.

Why do I make quilts? Every step of the way is an enjoyment. The process is rewarding, and as a teacher there is a need for me to pass it on and share. Perhaps you know me through the power of television, from my previous books, or from my years as a circuit rider in the quilt-teaching arena. For more than thirty years I did my best to teach quilting on PBS television. You may get tired of my voice, but with the show's reruns one never tires of refreshing the skills and methods.

So what happens when the camera stops? Well, quilt making goes on, teaching continues at a slower pace, and new interests emerge. Motivated by retreats, home-town "quilt groupies,"* and smaller classes, I have designed many new quilts to make and share. Retire? No way.

* *"Quilt groupies" are like-minded quilting friends who take turns meeting in welcoming homes to share and brag about their quilts. This is in contrast to larger groups (like guilds) with more regulations, officers, and dues.*

As I peruse the quilts I've made and taught during the last few years, they testify to all our classic shapes; squares, rectangles, triangles, diamonds, plus a new appliqué pattern. These have become the "how-to" quilts I share with you in *Scrap Happy Quilts*, along with my life stories.

Just like you, I've worn many hats as a teacher and quilter and have taken numerous paths along my journey. I've been a television host and author, teacher, quilt maker, collector, fabric designer, appraiser, merchant, inventor, quilt show attendee, guild member, groupie, judge, and circuit rider. This book explores the lessons learned from each of these, always benefiting from the mistakes.

Crossover quilts are what I call the creations that develop when sewing skills filter into other activities. In my life right now, that is exactly what happens.

For example, the Master Gardener program conducted through the County Home Extension service opens many new doors. The same diligence that goes into a quilt happens in an evolving garden. The same hands that create community quilts can help landscape the North Carolina State Playhouse grounds and even bring graphics to the outside walls. For me it is all about planning; gathering the tools, fabric, or plants; stitching and planting, together with the final process of quilting and watering. Don't forget the weeding and the unstitching!

Then, there are the hens! Something in my genetic makeup always had the yearning to keep chickens and reap their egg harvest. Even while living in the woods with other night creatures, I met the challenge. As chicken-keeping became more popular on a small scale, that led to the creation of another gathering group, our Hen Club, in Hendersonville.

Comedy/Tragedy Wooden Block at the North Carolina State Theater Playhouse. "All the world's a stage / And all the men and women merely players / They have their exits and their entrances" (William Shakespeare).

(Make this block in fabric on page 158.)

Miss Puff Ball on the Watering Can wall hanging,
by the author. 26" × 34".

When quilt groupies began to tease me about keeping hens, they just could not stop telling me things like this, which I call "Chick Power" phrases. Several come to mind, but they are endless!

Henpecked
Scarce as hen's teeth
Walking on eggshells
Pecking order
Mad as an old wet hen
Don't count your chickens until they are hatched
A chicken in every pot
Don't put all your eggs in one basket
Birdbrain
Birds of a feather flock together

My lifestyle, with its quilts and its cross-over quilts, revolves around our Quilt Built home. In our historic town of Flat Rock, North Carolina, the emphasis is on naming one's home; hence "Quilt Built" since many quilts hold up the walls. I eagerly share my secrets with all as I work on things like our "Toileaholic" dining room walls, on refinishing chairs, and on that special garden maze. What fun to pull out all the stops and decorate for pleasure and comfort. To share our home with family and friends is the best benefit.

So this book is a bit of a mix. A memoir, a celebration of the good times at home and on the road, and quilt patterns to keep you busy for a lifetime. Enjoy and get busy!

Being Scrap Happy

"*SCRAPS*: Fragments of material discarded as waste in manufacturing operations or made up of offs and ends; as a scrap dinner or, not in Webster's dictionary yet, a scrap quilt."

It has always pleased me to use up what would otherwise be discarded. Combine that idea with teaching people to quilt and I am one happy camper. We had a tradition in our family of making chop suey or Spanish rice with the leftover pork roast—sometimes better than the initial dinner. Being able to isolate and separate a variety of scrap fabric into a pieced or appliquéd design is so rewarding, leading to the point of true patchwork happiness.

"Waste not, want not" has become the mantra that echoes when making something special from otherwise throwaway fabric. That idiom, first recorded in 1772, suggests that if a person never wastes things, he or she will always have what is needed. Many years ago when my husband and I opened our Bonesteel Hardware & Quilt Corner Store in Hendersonville, North Carolina, a simple tip given to me at an International Quilt Market has led me to this collection of significant scrap quilts.

That tip was to cut off a yard of every new bolt of fabric that comes to the store and keep it as backup inventory. People would come in months later with their need for a little more of the fabric long after the bolt was gone, and we could help. Over twenty years of business, this array of choice, colorful fabric grew and expanded from our stock shelves to closets at home. It then finally prompted a move to a larger studio and home.

Little had I realized that once our store closed, this stockpile of fabric would result in an array of quilts and wall hangings.

The obvious question in your mind may be this: How to acquire scraps? If you haven't been making quilts over several years, just how do you get this stash? Here are some ways to start:

Beg from your quilt friends and "quilt groupies."

Haunt the quilt shops, with coupons in hand.

Visit the "next to new" shops, Humane Society, Goodwill, etc.

Check the internet for possibilities.

Decorators recycle textile samples. Make friends with your local decorators, so as to be there at the right time and place.

The Scrap Happy quilts presented here have been time-tested in classes, workshops, guilds, retreats, and my own Quilt Built studio. They are straightforward and easy for you to follow and build on. However, I do make the assumption for this book that you have sewing skills and have made at least one quilt, and that you have an understanding of fabric straight of grain, bias, and crosswise threads, plus rotary cutting skills.

After you enjoy some of the patterns here, if you're like many, you may want to keep going! Here are some ways to be a scrap happy person: sign up for a class at the local quilt shop, community college, or adult school; join a quilt guild; check out books at your local library (Dewey Decimal 742); and attend a course at a school for traditional and folk skills. Some schools to consider are:

The John C. Campbell Folk School
(www.folkschool.org)

Arrowmont School of Arts and Crafts
(www.arrowmont.org)

Penland School of Crafts (www.penland.org)

Haystack Mountain School of Arts
(www.haystack.org)

Sievers School of Fiber Arts
(www.sieversschool.com)

You can attend a quilt convention or symposium, start your own quilt group, and peruse the shows and videos available online.

To begin Scrap Happy quilting, I would suggest that you take a step back. Wherever you store your stash, leftover fabric, or mixed bag of scraps, get them all out to rearrange and organize. Pull them out from the closet, boxes in the basement, or their fancy studio storage. Refolding and color sorting will allow you to see the potential and where you might need to add more for a balance of color or design. I do this about once a year with much satisfaction.

Fondling the fabric is a special interaction with nostalgia. Where did it come from? Can I bear to cut it? Who was with me when I bought it? As these scraps do, many of the designs in *Scrap Happy Quilts* touch on the past and simpler times. Now, here is a chance to enjoy their nostalgia, using up-to-date methods with your very own stash. Keep in mind that what we create today becomes fiber history tomorrow. Forge ahead!

Backing amounts for each quilt and wall hanging are given for the various widths sold today: 45", 90", and 120" where applicable. However, there has been a trend to piece the backing fabric from leftovers from the front or from creative stash yardage, thus having a two-sided quilt.

Learn from yesterday, live for today,

hope for tomorrow.

—Albert Einstein

A task easily done leaves little satisfaction.

—GB

Family First

Our North Carolina Home

Just how did I get to this place in time? In terms of being at the right place at the right time, the praise really goes to my parents and their ancestors. Being born with a lot of energy, and the love of a simple needle and thread, added much to defining the direction I followed.

My resume begins in Sioux City, Iowa, July 21st, a day so hot that my mother always recalled, "They were frying eggs on the street." Our little family stayed in Iowa long enough to get a taste of cold weather and snow.

With a sister born in Miami, I always claimed that our home was anywhere between Iowa and Florida. Our father became an attorney with the Department of Justice, which meant relocating whenever a new case was tried. Our family lived in Iowa, Massachusetts, Texas, Florida, the District of Columbia, Kansas, and Illinois. All of this led to my attending 13 schools and two colleges, including Iowa State College, where I majored in clothing and textiles, and then Northwestern University, since I had a minor in the boy next door.

In 2006 I answered a call for quilts from Ami Simms to be part of "Alzheimer's: Forgetting Piece by Piece," a traveling quilt exhibit assembled to raise awareness and fund research. The exhibit was part of the Alzheimer's Art Quilt Initiative, a nonprofit that ultimately raised more than $1.1 million for Alzheimer's research.

Our father had some form of dementia, so driving had become an issue. My sister, Jill, met that challenge one very tearful day when she drove the car from North Carolina to Pennsylvania. My nephew now owns the car and the wall hanging (see page 17). Family stories are often cherished in quilts. (By the way, another classic story about our father was when he described his two daughters: "One is a famous world-traveling quilter on TV and the other one just steals cars!")

To keep me busy as a child, Mother would give me a box of hexagons with a needle and thread. It was slow going but eventually I figured out how to stop at those obtuse corners to get a perfect insert. I certainly think my great-grandmother, Charlotte (Lottie) Bradshaw Sayler, had determined the right way years before. Perhaps some talents, like stitchery, skip generations. My mother

Georgia, 18 months old. (Snowsuit made by Mother from an old coat.)

Georgia (five years old) and sister, Jill (one year old), 1941, Miami, Florida.

My mother, Virginia W. Jinkinson, holding 16-month-old me, 1938.

My father, Earl A. Jinkinson.

Left to right: Charlotte Bradshaw Sayler (Lottie), my great-grandmother; Pearl Watson, my grandmother; unidentified girl; Bernice Foltz, my aunt. Ca. 1899, Portage, Ohio.

sewed, out of need during the depression, but my grandmother only mended. I was fascinated watching my mother at the sewing machine. Once, at a lecture, I proudly introduced her in the audience, bragging that it was her love of sewing that led me on my career path. She candidly announced that she "really never liked to sew; it was a necessity during the Depression."

Lottie kept hens and had her own cows on the family farm. Delivering those eggs on horseback must have been a challenge, but well worth it if you had milk hanging in the saddlebags. By the end of the day she had butter. My mother often spent summers at the farm outside Portage, Ohio, and was given chores daily. Lottie did not appreciate idleness. If Mother was sitting she would say, "Go sweep the front walk," and Mother would reply, "I already did that." Lottie would say, "Yes, but a hen has since crossed the path." At Christmas, Mother would get a $5.00 bill from her. Lottie was the first woman in the county to drive a car.

To inherit a few of her quilt tops was special. The Job's Troubles quilt top was ignored for years mainly because of those jagged, difficult-to-bind edges. Once I set in a print triangle and added borders, it was ready to be quilted. It took three years, off and on, as I carried it everywhere with my lap hoop. Every time I quilted I wrote in a diary of what was happening in our lives; sometimes just the weather that day. The quilt and the diary will go to our first great-grandchild along with the blue ribbon won at the Asheville Quilt Show (www.ashevillequiltguild.org) in the two-person category.

As I quilted Lottie's quilt it occurred to me how difficult it would be to hand piece the top. It is the sort of quilt pattern that is continual and not just blocks put together. There are those eight obtuse angles where you only stitch up to the ¼" seam allowance, stop, and backstitch. I have included the pattern along with a schematic, but it is only for the serious and persistent quilter. You certainly have my permission to machine piece the top.

A Porsche Problem wall hanging. 35" × 35". It
commemorates a difficult family story, as explained
on page 15.

Lottie's Quilt (Job's Troubles)

71½" × 84½"

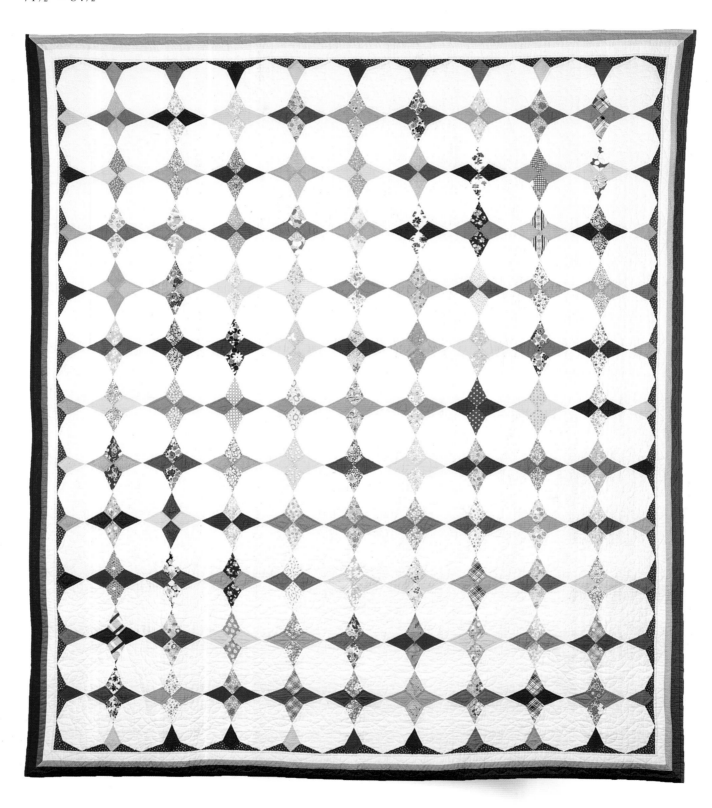

During the three years that I worked on this quilt, using the top that my great-grandmother Lottie made, I kept a diary of the other things that were happening in our family's life. Along with the blue ribbon it won at the Asheville Quilt Show, the quilt and the diary will be a gift to my first great-grandchild.

See the Patterns & Templates section for more.

Cutting:

Cut 99 pairs of A scrap fabric.

Cut 99 pairs of coordinated solid-color A plus 40 solid-color A for perimeter borders.

Cut 44 pairs of border ½ template A for outside set in borders.

Cut 120 light B template.

BORDERS:
(Note how I used three different shades of 4 colors for each border) 3¼" pieced borders

Inner light border: Cut 2 top and bottom 1 ¾" × 68½". Cut 2 side borders 1 ¾" × 81½".

Middle medium border: Cut 2 top and bottom 1¼" × 71". Cut 2 side borders 1¼" × 84".

Outside dark border: Cut 2 top and bottom 1 ¾" × 74¼". Cut 2 side borders 1 ¾" × 87½".

Method:

Sew the print/solid-fabric combination together. Use a variety of matching solids and prints.

1. For each scrap center sew the two halves together, stop, backstitch ¼" at outside obtuse point. With closed seams pressed, stagger the center connection always stopping, backstitch at the outside obtuse area. Create a twirl intersection on the center backside for a soft connecting seam.

2. Use a design wall or other flat surface to position colored sets for horizontal and vertical rows. Pin and set in the B background muslin fabric sewing just up to the quarter section. Build the quilt top in rows or in areas, referring to the layout often. Sticky notes help guiding the piecing process. Set in perimeter borders and corners as you stitch.

BINDING REQUIREMENTS:
9 yards of 2¼" wide cut fabric.

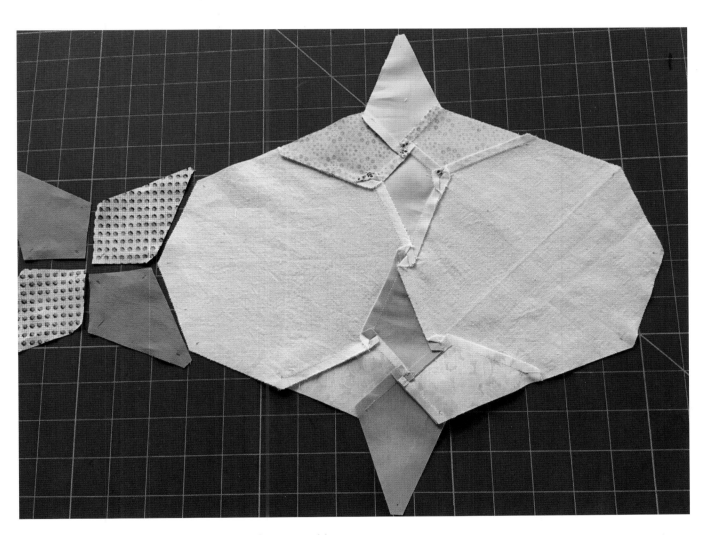

Sample in progress. Note ¼" markings and center twirl,
stopping and backstitching at obtuse angles.

Hummingbird Quilt

86" × 86"

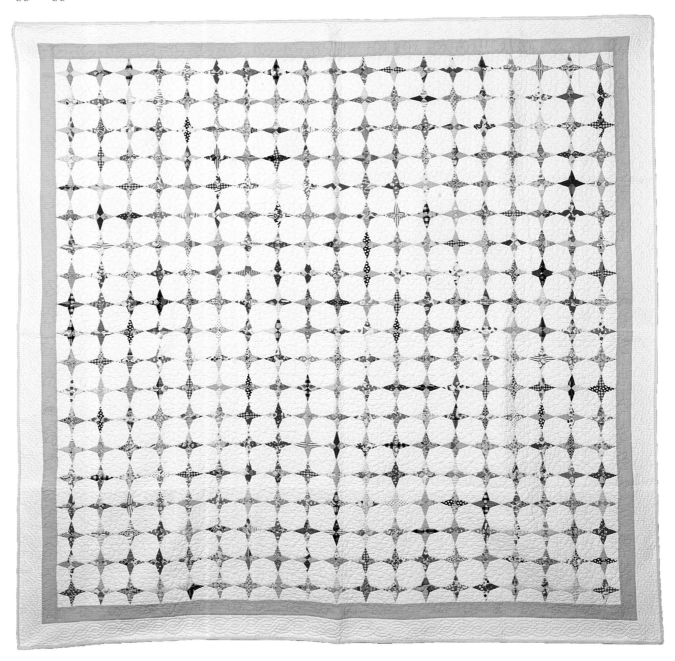

One day my friend Penelope Wortman came to a quilt get-together with another, simpler, version of Lottie's quilt. Penny is a lap quilter specializing in vintage, floral fabrics. She has had one of her quilts featured in all of my previous books. She even appeared on show 1006 of the *Lap Quilting* PBS television series. Penny's quilt is based on a 4" block, but I have added an alternate 6" block. Her quilt is total scrap with opposite prints the same, but without any solid-color accents.

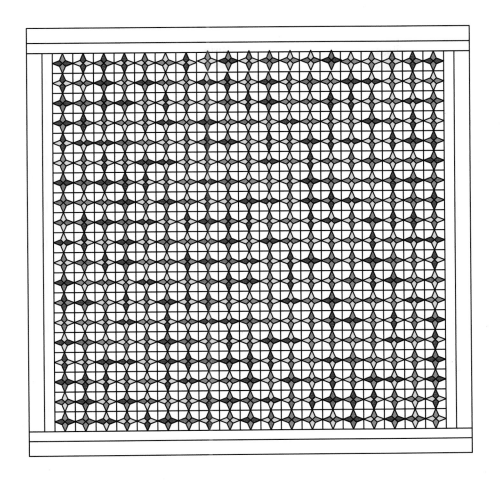

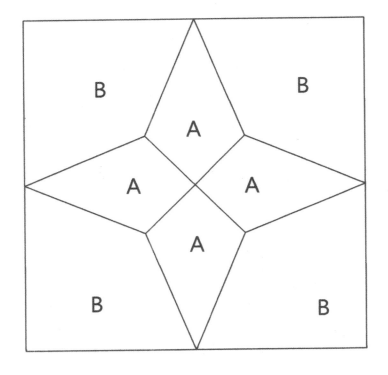

See the Patterns &
Templates section
for more.

Cutting:

4" block (19 rows of 19 blocks each yield a square quilt plus borders).

Cut 361 pairs of A print scrap templates 4". (Hint: Cut out duplicate prints at the same time.) Mark on the backside the ¼" turning end at each outside angle.

Cut 361 sets of 4 background fabrics. Mark on the backside the ¼" angle.

BORDERS:

Cut 2 side inner borders 2½" × 76½"

Cut 2 side outside borders 3½" × 76½"

Cut 2 top inner borders 2½" × 86½"

Cut 2 top outside borders 3½" × 86½"

Method:

The quilt consists of 19 blocks across with 19 rows, making a square quilt. Stitch one block at a time, enjoying the selection process.

On each fabric piece mark the ¼" points. Use a pin or pencil on the wrong side of the fabric. Sew the print A pieces together, stopping at the ¼" outside angle. Sew the two halves together with staggered closed seams. Release stitches at the center area up to the connecting seam for a twirl. This allows the center seam allowances to be twirled and makes for a soft intersection.

With a background piece, B, match points sewing from the outside up to the inside angle; stop and backstitch. Swing the print A around to the adjacent edge, sewing from the inside to the outside edge.

Continue with each of the other three B pieces until all are stitched.

Note on the backside how all closed seams can be pressed in a continuous manner. Continue sewing until all 361 blocks are complete. Arrange in rows with a pleasing balance of color.

Add borders.

The 6" blocks are sewn in the same manner but consist of 12 blocks across with 12 rows. 82" × 82".

Scraps:

Cut 144 pairs of A print templates (6")

Cut 144 of 4 background B template (6")

BORDERS:

Cut 2 side inner borders 2½" × 72½"; cut 2 outer side borders 3½" × 72½"

Cut 2 inner top borders 2½" × 82½"; cut 2 outer top borders 3½" × 82½"

BINDING REQUIREMENTS:
10 yards of 2¼" wide cut fabric.

Oh, so long ago. Note the wonderful sleeves. Wonder if any granddaughter will wear this?

Bonesteel family, 1968. (Left to right) Paul, 2; Jonathan, 6; Amy, 4.

My teenage years were spent babysitting, doing yard work, and flipping hamburgers at the Skokie Playfield/golf course in Wilmette, Illinois. After college my first real job was in the Fashion Office at Marshall Field & Co., the Old Orchard store. There I was closely working with fashion, fabric, mannequins, and real models. Soon I was creating the weekly fashion shows and writing the scripts for the narration.

Then marriage to Pete in 1959 and raising a family put a temporary halt to working outside the home with more moves from Illinois to Minnesota, Oklahoma, and eventually New Orleans. Desiring my own "egg money" found me taking in alterations, selling Avon door to door, and working for the Welcome Wagon. With Jonathan, Amy, and Paul in school full time it was time to use my sewing skills. Krauss Department store on Canal Street in the Quarter had a Saturday event where you would model a homemade garment with their fabric. It was a great promotional idea. The local WDSU television studio was looking for a sewing assistant for an in house series for Kenmore sewing machines through Sears & Roebuck. After the audition where I modeled my Vogue pattern ensemble, I got the job.

Imagine the fun stitching all sorts of garments and home decoration things for the star to use on her show. Well, they ran out of ideas for a show so I brought into the TV studio my home sewing, which included my husbands' neckties. Now, these were wide and polyester, but the rage at the time. Since there is always a nice triangle left over after cutting a bias cut tie pattern I made pillows and crazy-patch items. The star of the show, Terry Flettrich, mentioned upon seeing all of my stuff, "I wonder what my son-in-law does with the leftovers from his factory?" Well, my hands were shaking the day we opened those boxes. Tight layers of silk in various color ranges were all stacked just ready for creation. The key to my future was right there. So the combination of leftovers and limited television exposure set me on a path.

At work in the Fashion Office, circa 1960.

Vintage ensemble made in tones of
orange, but it got me the job!

It did take me several tries and rejects to come up with the best idea—little crazy-patch evening bags with lots of hand embroidery. The bags were limp until batting became the middle layer, putting body and shadows on the fabric surface. What fond memories I have of riding my bicycle on the Mississippi River levee, catching the free ferry and delivering our "Cajun Quilters" evening bags to boutiques.

In 1972 we moved to our final family destination. How wonderful to finally settle down. Living in the mountains of North Carolina really sparked an interest in quilts beyond little evening bags. The day we moved in, another neighbor was moving out but needed someone to take her sewing job at our community college. How perfect was that! After a couple of semesters I showed off my Cajun Quilter bags with a request to make big quilts. I was off and running, barely keeping ahead of my students weekly. Then came a suggestion from my mother to the effect of "Why not teach quilting on TV?" Nothing like that had been done before, so we filmed six how-to shows in 1976 in a simple studio at Swain Hall on the campus of UNC. These shows were so well received that we added seven more shows for a compete series of 13 that aired across the country starting in 1979.

My stimulus was directly related to my students and working hard to stay ahead of them. I am proud to say that in those early years our quilt class became the most filled on campus. We broke all records before computer classes emerged. Using a sewing machine for quilt

"Cajun Quilters" handbags sold in the French Quarter.

construction became acceptable. This does not take away from hand piecing, but I do believe if Great-Grandma had had a machine she would have used it for stronger tops done faster.

At the end of each 11-week session we would fill the auditorium with quilts and invite previous guests to "bring and brag" their completed projects. It was like contagious enthusiasm, and soon we had our own Western NC Quilters Guild in town. I am very proud to have been the first president. This was the time I was seriously cutting and stitching patchwork, often in duplicate—one for the actual class and quilt and another for TV. It was truly Quilting 101, with simple patterns using scissors and even cardboard templates. This was way before plastic templates, and the rotary cutter was just a dream away. Soon every *Lap Quilting* series got more progressive, using all the new tools invented. Magazines, symposiums, and travel outside my hometown meant more ideas.

Meeting some of the "movers and shakers" of the period was an inspiration. People who come to mind are Jinny Beyer, Jean Ray Laury, Carter Houck, Jeff Gutcheon, Donna Wilder, Yvonne Porcella, Chris Wolf Edmonds, and many more of that early period. We all have our mentors, and I tried hard not to copy but just be astounded at how quilt making was developing.

Never underestimate the power of TV. At first, when in front of the camera I tried very hard to instruct the camera crew. They had to really work with me to convince me that my "people" were in that tiny camera hole. It was during this time period that my books began being published to accompany and enhance the quilts I was making on TV. That first booklet, selling for $5.00, was hand-collated on our dining room table with the help of all three children. They soon tired of that, so I employed my mother and soon Norma, my secretary.

Television appearances led to visiting guilds, conventions, and various teaching engagements that opened up my creative juices. The mingling and interactions with

fellow quilters helped me develop different titles and show ideas. My praise goes to Bill Hannah, the producer of *Lap Quilting*, for never questioning my topics, and to our loyal sponsors for 12 series of 13 half-hour shows. Early on they did inform me that the makeup artist and the wardrobe people were on vacation. It was up to me, so I had fun coming up with some pretty bizarre, outlandish garments. For the last series I wore the same blue western shirt with a decorated bib (or "breastplate," as my UK friend Sheila named it) for each of the 13 shows.

I was so totally entrenched and thrilled with what I was doing that it did not seem at the time like a movement. I was obsessed, and somehow fit in around the quilting some family, hiking, tennis, and home-scene maintainence. All of a sudden writing more books and

Decorated bibs for the *Lap Quilting* XII series on PBS, produced by UNC-TV.

My books.

operating Bonesteel Hardware & Quilt Corner became part of our lives.

A trip to England opened up new doors when I visited Foyle's Book Store to observe an exhibit of Pauline Burbidge's work and art. Patchwork pictures were a new concept to me, and I was privileged to finally actually take a class from her where she taught strip picture piecing in Washington, DC, at the Continental Quilt Congress run by Hazel Carter. Other stimulating quilt opportunities were the *Quilters Newsletter* magazine, the Good Housekeeping quilt contest, and the *Baltimore Quilt* event, where I judged my first big show.

So the next 35 years were busy times—filming 13-week television series every other year for University of North Carolina Public TV and writing companion books. I have been blessed with some great publishers, editors, and photographers. People still come up to me, bragging on having their original copy of my paperback booklet. We all have to start someplace, since there is no doubt we crawl before we walk. I found that a visual how-to on television leads to confidence and the "I can do it" attitude. Then to clarify the process in books makes it a reality for learners.

Creative clutter is better than idle neatness.

—*GB*

live and learn

The Quilt Maker and Designer

I have learned that you seldom build the perfect house, so why expect to make the perfect quilt. (With the exception of a masterpiece quilt that many wish to attain.) Maybe that is why we keep making quilts—to finally get it right. As teachers we boast that patchwork should not be cast in stone and changes are acceptable, to form a stepping-stone to creativity. My mantra has always been "A task easily done leaves little satisfaction."

When it comes to designing, many factors come into play. Twelve pieced lines converging at one intersection spells trouble with a capital T or time with a capital T. We are now making calculator quilts. If only our math teachers had schooled us in fabric, we would have been steps ahead in our field. It all comes down to one's desire to achieve the final goal—fabric and pattern selection, cutting out, piecing, and quilting.

Quilts often become testimonies to life's frustrating experiences. My "Seeing Stars" quilt is just that. It was my entry into the Statue of Liberty contest, my year quilt that challenged me with new star angles, and the quilt I took to the hospital when I had my surgery in 1985; so it was special. Our congressman, Charles Taylor, somehow saw it and due to its patriotic colors requested it to hang in his Washington, DC, offices. Yes, I was flattered to show it in our nation's capital. Then, as I prepared for a European teaching and filming trip, I could not find my passport. We tore the house apart, checking under rugs, at the bank, and in all the drawers in the house, but to no avail. It was the weekend before my flight, and I was told I could leave the country but shouldn't expect to return to the USA without a passport.

What to do? Call your congressman. So all weekend I pestered his office and was finally told it was hopeless.

I was packed, ready to go, when I just happened to search again in the little cubbyhole deep down in the desk where it was supposed to be. There it was! How foolish I felt. So much so that upon my return I gave my "Seeing Stars" quilt to Charles Taylor. Plus I gave my antique desk, circa 1963, Minneapolis Salvation Army Store, to a resale shop. Lesson learned: Keep track of your passport. Do you know where yours is right now?

My patchwork life is like woven fabric—the warp, those strong threads first applied to the loom that run parallel to the selvage, called the straight of the grain, is my strength. It's my husband, our children, my sister, my health, my work ethic, and those inherited genes. The woof or crosswise threads weave in and out and become the character and mix that pulls the fabric together. Here, think my Bernina, color, and the notions and toys we depend on, plus those eager students.

What used to be made only by hand has taken on a new character and level of acceptance. In the end, I have learned that all quilters are control conscious. We might not be able to control some things in our lives, like the weather, taxes, or what happens tomorrow, but we can take charge of our quilt process and get lost in patchwork.

Learn from the new quilt patterns offered here in *Scrap Happy*.

They are based on our basic principles but push the design elements, using new methods. Use up that "stash" knowing there is more out there to tease the pocketbook.

WHAT I LEARNED:

I appreciate the evolution of quilt making from scissors and cardboard templates to calculator and rotary cutter quilts. With the right guidance and gumption you can make a quilt.

The Quilt Collector

I have learned that it is not smart to collect quilts if you have only four beds. However, there are exceptions to this rule. As a beginning teacher I became obsessed with patterns and old quilt tops. Before I realized it the closets were filling up with quilts, some just tops.

The quilts I acquired were used as props on the TV set, inspiration for new quilts, teaching examples, and décor in our home. Some were just cherished for being made.

But there comes a time when space determines relocation.

An antique fair find. 86" × 90".

A collection of three antique quilts now resides in the Charleston Museum that had notable names and dates placing them made in the area. Going behind the scenes at museums is very revealing as to the storage and care of antique quilts. Recalling visits to the Shelburne Museum in Vermont, Winterthur in Delaware, and the Smithsonian in DC gave me a sincere appreciation for quilt conservation. I learned it takes space, time, a devoted staff, and money.

Discovering a unique house quilt top on Main Street at an antique fair resulted in a summer coverlet. The pattern gave me the idea for a small wall hanging that would be made by the Cover Lovers for a member who moved to another state. Quilts are not only for remembering but for reliving their making.

As a proficient quilter and collector, one never knows when that collection will be called upon. Sometimes a family tragedy can fill in the gaps. When our son's family home burned down along with twelve of my quilts, I was able to replenish part of their collection.

Finally, I have the time to do justice to all the quilts I have made and acquired; a proper inventory. With a proper computer list I can record names, a description, date made, and value. To complete this assessment each quilt must have a label.

WHAT I LEARNED:
Savor historic quilts, learn from them, share them with others, store them properly, and ultimately find them a home.

A gift for a faraway Cover Lover, Barb Pliner. 36" × 36".

The Fabric Designer

Oh, what fun to see your name on the selvage of fabric. At a certain time period in our fabric history, having a name on the edge of fabric became very popular and signified that you were an authentic quilter. This naming was more than the business associated with a line of fabric; all of a sudden, actual quilters were having their own line of fabric. For me, it meant a trip down to the mill, where the strike-off was done and actual yardage was printed. Seeing this process prompted my curiosity to explore our entire cotton production. Hence, I made an entire 30-minute *Lap Quilting* episode devoted to cotton, called "From Field to Fabric," where we opened in a cotton field and proceeded to show and describe each step along the way.

Yes, I did covet those silly printed selvages. It was hard to throw them away. Finally, I decided to enhance a denim jacket with those ends, along with some beads. It was tedious and required a crochet hook to pull those narrow fabric threads through the beads. So, once again, I employed my mother. Well, in the process, she left the crochet hook near my father's chair, where he always kept his toothpick, and you guessed it, he got the crochet hook caught in his teeth and exclaimed, "Call 911." Naturally, they got it out it out and she was able to finish!

Another fabric opportunity came with my involvement with the Quilters Hall of Fame in Marion, Indiana. Honoring Marie Webster with a line of fabric resulted in a lovely collection plus a clever baby quilt depicting many beds.

It was an honor to become a Quilters Hall of Fame Honoree in 2003 with several trips back to Marion, Indiana, at other celebrations. Bonesteel Films along with UNC TV produced a one-hour special, *The Great American Quilt Revival*, which is still available for viewing (on Vimeo, search for it by title). To further enhance their monetary bank I created a wonderful autograph quilt where signatures were sold, and we included all the notable previous honorees. It is now in the permanent collection of the Quilters Hall of Fame (www.quilters

Denim jacket full of beaded selvages.

halloffame.net) thanks to the Ardis James family. Make your own autograph quilt along with easy shams for the pillows (page 92).

Picking out a favorite of Marie Webster's quilt was easy to do once I perused the Sunflower quilt. I have adapted the quilt to a combination of piecing for the stems and machine appliqué for the flowers. What makes it special is the machine lap assembly, allowing the blocks to be done separately and then put together (page 134).

Today's quilter has become very keen on fabric collections. They seek out certain lines, search more out on the internet, create designs based on name brands, and hoard certain batiks. So, we all praise the fabric designers: long may they design and print.

WHAT I LEARNED:

I have since learned many other practical uses for those selvages. They are great for tying up rolled quilt bundles and for crocheting into rugs, and even can be string pieced into quilt blocks.

Baby quilt made with the Marie Webster collection
by Georgia Bonesteel; Windham Fabrics. 42" × 56".

The Appraiser

What is in a name? When it comes to quilts it becomes mandatory that it be given its rightful name or category. That somehow makes it legal and verifies its existence. For years, when owning our Bonesteel Hardware & Quilt Corner, I would counsel people when they appeared with the family quilt. I will always recall spreading out a crazy-patch quilt on our old glass/wooden case, and upon inspection finding Eleanor Roosevelt's and Will Rogers's inked autographs. That made it special, plus it was then museum worthy. Directing an antique quilt back to the area where it was made is always a good idea if the museum has the funds to preserve it properly.

To this day we all refer to Barbara Brackman's *Encyclopedia of Pieced Quilt Patterns* for reference, design options, and naming a pattern. For more legal verification of a quilt for insurance purposes, a professional certified appraiser is necessary. Then pattern name, fiber content, age, photography, and family research are documented.

WHAT I LEARNED:
Quilt identification can be a challenge and rewarding, often left to the professionals.

The Merchant

We learned to do many things owning Bonesteel Hardware & Quilt Corner for 20 years, located in our hometown, Hendersonville, North Carolina. In fact, we were proud to know that we were second only to Connemara, the Carl Sandburg Home, for the most visited spot in town.

When I had my first job out of college it was for Marshall Field & Company in Chicago, and their mantra was "The customer is always right," which we carried on into our business. What do you look for in a business? High-quality fabric offered at competitive prices, eager employees to assist and handle your needs plus inspiration with classes, and, naturally, quilts on the walls. Hand holding, engaging the customer in classes, and making them dependent on your store is a must.

Yardstick holder for thread or thimbles.

I learned there is a fine line between guilds and the local quilt store. The motto is this: Promote but not pushy. Today it is a joy to see successful shops and compare how they succeed with a lot of work. Not operating a store any longer makes me appreciate even more the personal connection we had with people. Yes, it is true that employees will walk you through the many steps in quilt making and guide you to the right books, notions, and tools, along with fabric and even the essential sewing machine. Many days I miss that experience.

We were proud to have our own wooden yardsticks to hand out to customers until we realized they were disappearing too fast. Soon I was made aware of a novelty thread holder made from four of our yardsticks selling at local fairs. Pretty clever, but we then decided to put a price of 50 cents for each yardstick. Sure cut their overhead!

WHAT I LEARNED:

There is more to operating a quilt store than just loving quilts. One must have business savvy and the desire to make a profit. There comes a time, however, to savor life away from business.

The Inventor

As I write this, a new gizmo is being invented, and if you have an idea you'd better patent it yesterday. I have learned that it costs money to make money, so be as clever and swift as you can. Early in my television career I became associated with a simple little chatelaine worn around my neck. At one end was a square pocket made from two cathedral quilt squares that held thread and needles, while a thread cutter hung on the other end.

Sometimes even lingo became an invention, such as referring to my "dog ears," those clipped off triangles from patchwork. We develop trademarks that tend to stay without teaching. As I explored appliqué I saw a need for a light box, so I developed a simple, foldaway box that supported an acrylic top. All one needed was an under-the-counter light inside. These boxes had a limited life span as newer ones hit the market.

Discovering the flexible curve was another notion bonus. As a drafting tool it had been around for ages; even ship navigators used these with maps. They can always be found in college bookstores in various lengths. But developing a method to sew and flip curves became a new class that led to exciting landscape quilts.

One can never bank on the longevity of a product, either. If I showed something really special, like a needle tracker, for the sewing machine, there is every reason that it would evaporate by the time the show was in the rerun mode. How disappointing for the customer. However, the sewing-machine industry got the message, so that now you can actually program what needle you have in the machine each time you are stitching, or rely on color-coded needle tops.

Once I learned to "rock and roll" quilt, I became very dependent on the indented thimble. Soon many others discovered this unique quality of being able to lock in the eye of the needle in that groove at the end of a thimble for hand quilting.

One day someone mentioned that freezer paper adheres to fabric with a dry iron. The lightbulb clicked in my head. Plastic templates would be a thing of the past. Being able to print a continuous quarter-inch grid on freezer paper certainly opened up doors for many. Now, we have a graph pad along with templates. At first I convinced a freezer paper company in Parchment, Michigan (of all places!), to print this grid, but they are in the food industry and could not quite market the product successfully, even after I told them that it was an advantage to measure the amount of frozen foods. Soon I was printing Grid Grip and teaching its potential. Years later, I added to the printing with sheets of equilateral triangles.

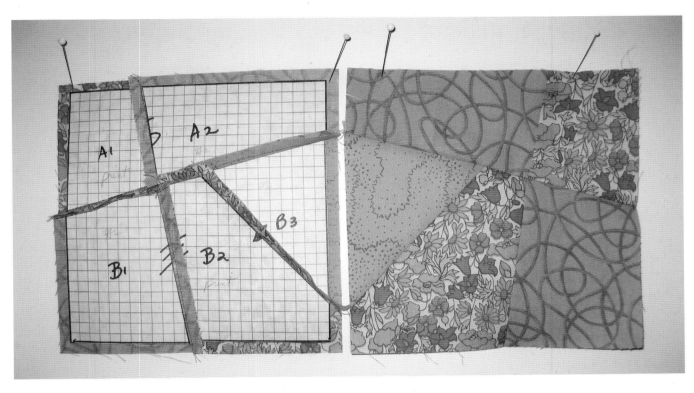

Angled four-patch with Grid Grip used as a stitching line.

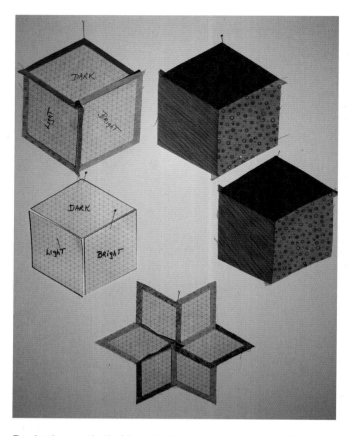

Designing and stitching 60-degree diamonds such as Baby Blocks.

Revisiting a hexagon class taken years ago awakened all the possibilities for this classic shape as it applies to stars, tumbling blocks, and much more. Even teachers can learn something when they take a class. When new techniques are learned, the important thing is to make them your own with original patterns, always crediting the source.

The quilt public is always eager for something new and different. It can be as simple as a basket liner. We live in peach and apple country here, so the baskets are plentiful. Once I figured out how to make a liner, the pattern sold like hot cakes.

Another time at a retreat a quilter complained about scissor-cutting layers of fabric between narrow stitching lines. She was in the garment business working on vests and jackets, but her hands were hurting. It occurred to me that if strips of narrow green mat could slip in between those sewn lines, she could use a rotary cutter. Next time I went to the Quilt Market I wondered why people were in a long line shopping at the Omnigrid booth. You guessed it—they were buying Omnistrips—cutting mats for Faux Chenille.™ Guess my phone tip paid off for them!

One of the most inventive aspects of the quilt world recently has been Blocks on Barns for quilt trails. Find your favorite block on a barn wall hanging and use freezer paper for making the pattern.

WHAT I LEARNED:

Any new idea, notion, or method requires research and diligence. Go fast with resolve for a patent, copyright, or trademark.

For the Bay Berry Quilt Guild, 2010, named "One of 26."
30" × 27".

The Judge / The Contestant

I have learned that a ribbon or an award is an extension of self-worth. This experience comes from judging many shows, but also being on the receiving end. I recall judging a show with Jean Ray Laury in Houston and giving an award to a quilt called "Three Dog Night." I knew it was the name of a music group, but more important I discovered that it referred to the number of dogs needed in bed to stay warm. I enter shows not so much for the ribbon, but to brag on completion. To have a quilt recognized by peers is always special. What a thrill to have Ruth McDowell honor me with a judge's choice for my "Masks, Moose and Qupak" quilt from *Bright Ideas for Lap Quilting.*

Judges can be fickle, so enter your quilts in more than one show. Go ahead, be brave and read the judges' critique, as they have evaluated all aspects of your quilt against the rest of the field. These tips can help you go forward and make improvements. The quilts I have made over the years have always been teaching tools for books and television or the classroom. For them to find their place on a bed for warmth is an added bonus for our family.

WHAT I LEARNED:

Enter a judged show as a positive step in quilt making. Even if you are not a judge, volunteer as a scribe.

Collection of ribbons/name tags.

The Quilt Show

You can rent a college auditorium; lease the Brown Convention Center in Houston, Texas, where the International Quilt Festival is held; drop quilts onto folding chairs placed on top of six-foot tables; or even have the honor of exhibiting your quilt at the National Quilt Museum, and they will come. Do they come for a quilt viewing, or is it the merchants that lure the public? Either way it becomes the combination of many hands and minds at work.

Going to a quilt show can be such a learning experience. What are the latest trends? Do you want to sell your quilt? That could lead to buying more fabric. Just about every show today has a demonstration area to learn new methods. Sometimes it can be an eye opener and even make one feel intimidated by the show of excellence, ribbons, and new patterns. It is better to think positive and ponder, "Maybe next year, so get busy!" Ideas abound at shows, so even if you have not made a quilt it will prompt you to take a class and just dive in to the prospect of stitching. These shows conducted by groups of guild members or businesses develop strong work ethics and new friendships along the way. I am proud to say that I was chairperson of two North Carolina State Quilt Symposiums at Kanuga Conference in Hendersonville, North Carolina. Work? You can be sure the rewards were well worth the effort. A lasting reminder is a special quilt that still hangs there after all these years, designed by Betsy Freeman.

For many quilters, going to these events has become an annual migration. So many memories flood back from these shows: men at one booth wearing skirts (this brought a lot of attention); booths with stacks of feed sacks (where did they all come from?); finding new ways with the old, like the transition from scissors to rotary cutter to fabric cutting dies; or entire quilt groups wearing identical vests. I became dependent on these conventions to fuel topics for each new *Lap Quilting* series.

The fall of 2001, with the New York City tragedy, was an auspicious time for the International Quilt Association show in Houston. It carried on in style, paying tribute using the best way quilters can express themselves—with quilts. That was the year I received the Silver Star Salute along with a memorable pin depicting a TV screen. Adding to my other accolades, of which I am very proud, is my 2002 Bernina of America Award, my 2003 Hall of Fame induction, and in 2015, my Legend of the Year for the Quilt Show, putting an age factor onto my quilt life. But that should not slow me or you down!

WHAT I LEARNED:

Shows are a culmination of classes and hours of quilting with an opportunity to compare, compete, buy, and enjoy.

Kanuga Conference quilt, 54" × 85". The Western North Carolina Quilter's Guild members who worked on it are Mary Berry, Betsy Freeman, Ann Kanipe, Kathy Willis, Mary Ruth Branyon, Martine House, Georgia Bonesteel, Peggy Genuine, Bernie Sickler, Kitty Howell, Velma Everhart, Mary Lattimore, June Haynes, Jan Zimmerman, and Gail Baer.

Life without industry is guilt;

industry without art is brutality.

—John Ruskin

The Geometrics

The scrap quilts offered here pay homage to our classic geometrics. Given our rotary cutter, speed cutting and rulers adapting measurements to fabric is a piece of cake. After all, we have 360 degrees offered but depend mostly on the 45, 60, and 90 degrees for these shapes. When we wander off these lines, more-creative picture designs evolve.

Crazy Patch Splashes Quilt

94" × 94"

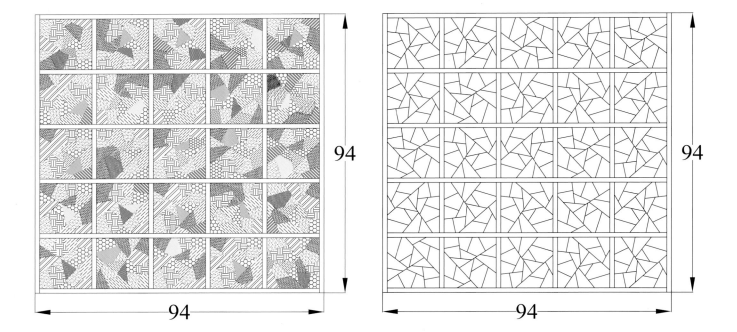

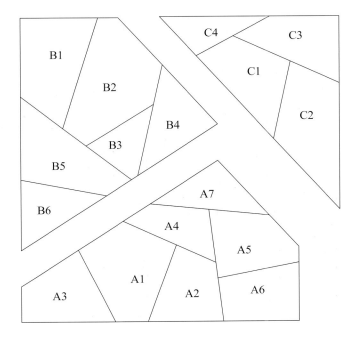

Gather your black and white scrap fabrics, plus add a splash of color for this updated crazy patch quilt. One square of gridded freezer paper, Grid Grip, makes a row of five blocks repeated five times to make 25 blocks.

Fabric:

Select a theme color or a medley of all your scraps, using 10 to 16 different fabrics for each block. Add an accent color splash for each block, knowing that repeats are allowed.

Method:

Cut a 17' square of gridded freezer paper (Grid Grip). Pencil in angle lines. (Store-bought freezer paper can be used, but indicate random grain lines in several areas on the square.) Try to keep templates about the same size to avoid seam intersections. Develop three main sections and remember that each line drawn is a seam. One pattern is all you need, since the fabric changes in each block and each block will be turned to balance shades and angle lines.

Code each template according to piecing sequence. Within the three sections label templates A1, A2, etc. Add crossover clues between templates as an arrow, dash lines, or waves. Take a picture with an iPhone or iPad for later reference.

Cut the paper template apart with a rotary cutter. Select five fabrics and five accent fabrics for each of the templates. Stack these fabrics according to grain line and cross grain. Start with A1 by pressing (shiny, polycoated side down) the template onto the right side, allowing excess fabric on all sides, matching grain lines with the paper grid. With a ruler and rotary cutter, add ¼" on all sides. Proceed with each of the templates, including the color splash template.

The Grid Grip can also be pressed onto the backside of the layered fabric, but it will reverse the image.

With one row pressed and seam allowances added, start piecing with A1 to A2, then A3, etc. Pin and peek by folding back the seam allowance to match paper points and edges. Pin in place for the accurate ¼" seam allowance. Do not stitch into the paper edges, as these templates are used four more times. Move on to section B and then section C. Sew sections A, B, and C together to make one block. Blocks should measure 17½" square.

Repeat the above to make a total of 25 blocks. Grid Grip can be reironed many times. Once all the blocks are completed, a design wall or bed top aids in placement of the rows to balance color and fabrics.

Arrange each of the five rows of blocks in a balanced, pleasing manner. Stitch five blocks and four connector rectangles together to make one row. Repeat step #4 to make five rows. Sew rows together with four strips in between the rows as shown and complete with outside borders.

BORDER CUTS:
Yardage required: 1⅔ yards

BINDING REQUIREMENTS:
10½ yards of 2¼" wide cut fabric.

Cut 20 rectangles 2" × 17½" (connectors between blocks)

Cut 6 strips 2" × 91½" (between rows plus top and bottom)

Cut 2 strips 2" × 94½" (side borders)

This quilt was longarm quilted by Debbie Beaver.

Several completed blocks, Grid Grip pattern,
and Rosie, our cat.

Squares:
The Real Trip Around the World Quilt

76½" × 85½"

This classic quilt pattern takes on a new, easier method thanks to the rotary cutter and precut lengths. What used to be one patch at a time can now gain momentum through quick cutting the daunting 54 fabrics. It is offered in three sizes: full quilt, medium, and a smaller version.

Not only have I taught The Real Trip Around the World in many places, but a special request made it "worldly." Jeni Hankins literally sang for scraps. Prior to class at the John C. Campbell Folk School she toured England musically and exchanged a CD for fabric. So each of her squares represented another "gig." Our class treat was a noontime serenade.

FIRST STEP: CUTTING DIAGRAM #1

Length(s) of 2" Wide Strips Required per Color

#	Mat'l	#	Mat'l	#	Mat'l	#	Mat'l
1	2"	15	8",40"(2),24"	29	4",24",40"(4),16"	43	32",40",24"
2	8"	16	8",40"(2),32"	30	16",40"(4),24"	44	24",40",24"
3	8",8"	17	8",40"(3)	31	8",40"(4),24"	45	16",40",24"
4	8",16"	18	8",40"(3),8"	32	40"(4),24"	46	8",40",24"
5	8",24 "	19	8",40"(3),16"	33	32",40"(3),24"	47	40",24
6	8",32"	20	8",40"(3),24"	34	24",40"(3),24"	48	32",24"
7	8",40"	21	8",40"(3),32"	35	16",40"(3),24"	49	24",24"
8	8 ",40 ",8 "	22	8",40"(4)	36	8",40"(3),24"	50	16",24"
9	8",40",16"	23	8",40"(4),8"	37	40"(3),24"	51	8",24"
10	8",40",24"	24	8",40"(4),16"	38	32",40"(2),24"	52	24"
11	8",40",32"	25	8",40"(4),24"	39	24",40"(2),24"	53	16"
12	8",40"(2)	26	8",40"(4),32"	40	16",40"(2),24"	54	8"
13	8",40"(2),8"	27	4",40"(5)	41	8",40"(2),24"		
14	8",40"(2),16"	28	4",32",40"(4),8"	42	40"(2),24"		

Diagram 1, Large.

Length(s) of 2" Wide Strips Required per Color

#	Mat'l	#	Mat'l	#	Mat'l	#	Mat'l
1	2"	15	8",40"(2),24"	29	24",40"(2),32"	43	24"
2	8"	16	8",40"(2),32"	30	16",40"(2),32"	44	16"
3	8",8"	17	8",40"(3)	31	8",40"(2),32"	45	8"
4	8",16"	18	8",40"(3),8"	32	40"(2),32"		
5	8",24"	19	8",40"(3),16"	33	32",40"(2),32"		
6	8",32"	20	8",40"(3),24"	34	24",40"(2),32"		
7	8",40"	21	8",40"(3),32"	35	16",40"(2),32"		
8	8",40",8"	22	4",40"(4)	36	8",40",32"		
9	8",40",16"	23	4",32",40"(3),8"	37	40",32"		
10	8",40",24"	24	4",24",40"(3),16"	38	32",32"		
11	8",40",32"	25	4",16",40"(3),24"	39	24",32"		
12	8",40"(2)	26	8",40"(3),32"	40	16",32"		
13	8",40"(2),8"	27	40"(3),32"	41	8",32"		
14	8",40"(2),16"	28	32",40"(2),32"	42	32"		

Diagram 1, Medium.

Length(s) of 4¼" Wide Strips Required per Color

#	Mat'l	#	Mat'l	#	Mat'l
1	4 ¼"	8	17", 51"(2)	15	17", 51", 34",
2	17"	9	17", 51"(2), 17"	16	51", 34"
3	17", 17"	10	8 1/2", 51"(2),34"	17	34"(2)
4	17", 34"	11	8 1/2", 34", 51"(2)	18	17", 34"
5	17", 51"	12	8 1/2", 17"(2), 51"(2)	19	34"
6	17"(2), 51"	13	51"(2), 34"	20	17"
7	17", 51", 34"	14	34"(2), 51"		

Diagram 1, 4¼ inches.

Length(s) of 3" Wide Strips Required per Color

#	Mat'l	#	Mat'l	#	Mat'l
1	3"	8	12", 36"(2)	15	12", 36", 24",
2	12"	9	12", 36"(2), 12"	16	36", 24"
3	12", 12"	10	6", 36"(2),24"	17	24"(2)
4	12", 24"	11	6", 24", 36"(2)	18	12", 24"
5	12", 36"	12	6", 12", 36"(2), 12"	19	24"
6	12", 36", 12"	13	36"(2), 24"	20	12"
7	12", 36", 24"	14	24", 36", 24"		

Diagram 1, Small.

Refer to Diagram 1 for the fabric cuts, 2" wide for the large and medium, 4¼" and 3" for smaller versions, but varying lengths.

A few tips:

Select fabrics with random abandon, cutting 54 different fabrics. Other sizes have different amounts. Keep selected fabric available in case of issues after sewing begins.

If you want a color wave, choose similar shaded fabrics next to each other.

Each # is a different color, but varying lengths in order of how they are sewn, with some colors having more cuts as #12 (2) cuts 40", and #33 requires (3) lengths 40", etc.

The 8" and three 4" cuts are the connector strips that set the rest of the quilt. Each section sewn, cut apart, and restitched is a mirror image of each other—all done in sections, which are the fabric bands. (D5)

Crosswise cuts, selvage to selvage, work best to get the 40" length.

Fat quarters or remnants can be pieced.

A magazine with sticky notes works well to keep the cuts in order so that each turned page contains a new color with varying lengths.

As you make your cuts, inserting them between pages, also make a swatch runner. Pin and then stitch very small fabric swatches to a strip of torn selvage, leaving room to number each color. These will represent the order of your strips and prevent any "unpicking" or use of seam ripper. You will check this often.

Do not stress over fabric selection. I have never seen an ugly quilt from any of the many Real Trip Around the World tops. They all respond to the beauty of fabrics. It is the repetition of squares that create an ever-expanding diamond that is so appealing.

Always sew on the same sewing machine for a consistent ¼" seam allowance.

Gather some friends to make this quilt over a period of several weeks.

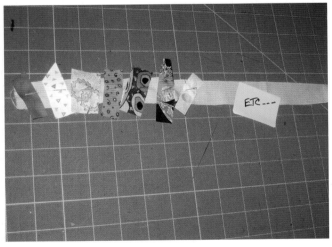

SECOND STEP: PIECING AND PRESSING CONNECTORS

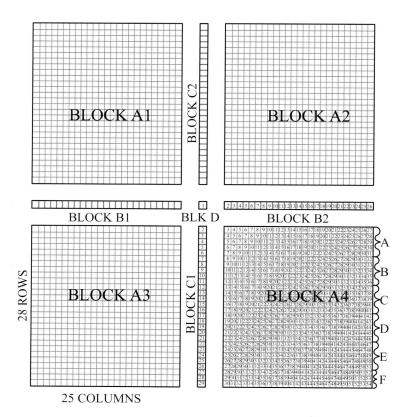

Diagram 2, Large.

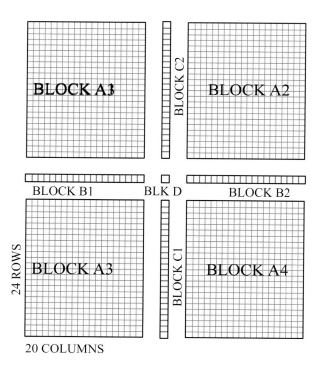

Diagram 2, Medium.

Block Diagram

Finished size: 63¾" × 86¼"

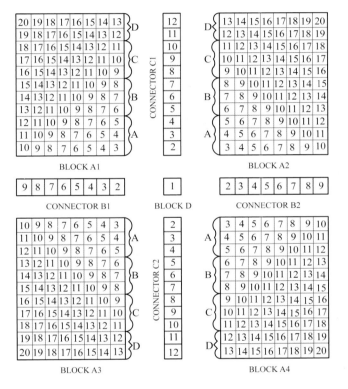

Diagram 2, 4¼ inches.

Block Diagram

Finished size: 42½" × 57½"

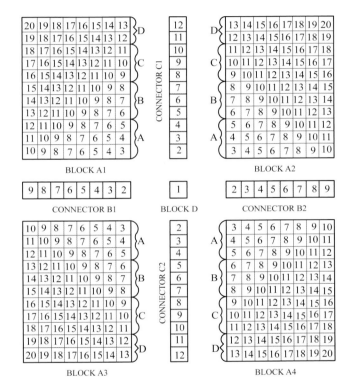

Diagram 2, Small.

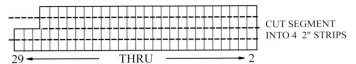

CUT SEGMENT
INTO 4 2" STRIPS

29 ← ——— THRU ——— → 2

2" × 4" strips of fabrics #27–#29 for C1 & C2
2" × 8" strips of fabrics #2–#26 for B1, B2, C1 & C2

Diagram 3, Large.

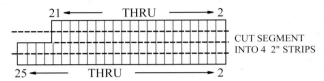

21 ← ——— THRU ——— → 2

CUT SEGMENT
INTO 4 2" STRIPS

25 ← ——— THRU ——— → 2

2" × 4½" strips of fabrics #21–#25 for C1 & C2
2" × 8½" strips of fabrics #2–#21 for B1, B2, C1 & C2

Diagram 3, Medium.

First Assembly of Connectors B1, B2, C1 & C2

Colors 2 through 12

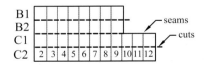

4¼" × 17" strips of fabrics #2–#9 for B1, B2, C1 & C2
4¼" × 8½" strips of fabrics #10–#12 for C1 & C2

Cut the assembly into four 4¼" wide bands

Diagram 3, 4¼ inches.

First Assembly of Connectors B1, B2, C1 & C2

Colors 2 through 12

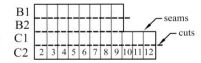

3" × 12" strips of fabrics #2–#9 for B1, B2, C1 & C2
3" × 6" strips of fabrics #10–#13 for C1 & C2

Cut the assembly into four 3" wide bands

Diagram 3, Small.

Diagram 2 presents the overall schematic of the large quilt. Each quarter section is a mirror image, with Blocks B and Blocks C called the connectors.

Pin the connectors together, #2 color through #26 color, adding the #4" cuts that go to #29. Stitch these together.

On the backside lightly press the closed seams in alternate directions, out and then in, for the longer C section. This pressing is NOT how we used to do it by directing rows in opposite directions. Alternate the closed seams to be pressed toward each other (innies) and next to that pressed outward (outies). Cut the C section apart every 2". Then press the shorter B section in opposite directions, in and then out closed seams. Cut apart every 2".

Firmly press these rows on the front side, pressing out any lip or overhang areas, and position on a flannel design wall, which will divide the segments. A sheet spread on a bed works also for a design area. Alternating these seams will make it possible to twirl all intersections eventually. See Diagram 2, where "innie" and "outie" seams are noted. This releasing and twirling of intersections results in a soft, flat connection.

Layout of connectors pinned, but not sewn.

THIRD STEP: PIECING AND PRESSING BLOCKS

Once the connectors are cut and pieced, arrange them according to Diagram 2. Cut the center square according to the quilt size, and put it in place for connection after the four sections are completed. Sometimes the color choice will change once the remainder of the quilt is sewn.

Quilt Size	Center Square Size
Large	2"
Medium	2"
Georgia's College Quilt	4¼"
Trip Around the Ranch	3"

Diagram 4.

Strips for Blocks A1–A4

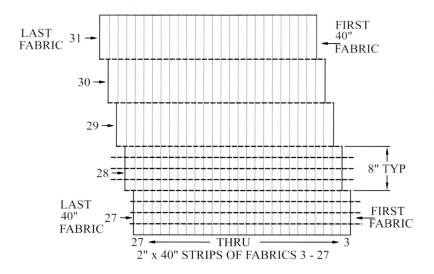

Cut each segment into four 2" strips
Reassemble one strip from each segment into blocks A1–A4

Diagram 5, Large.

Strips for Blocks A1–A4

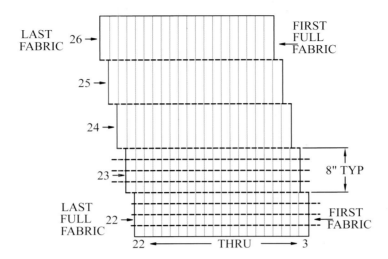

Cut each segment into four 2" strips
Reassemble one strip from each segment into blocks A1–A4

Diagram 5, Medium.

Strips for Blocks A1–A4

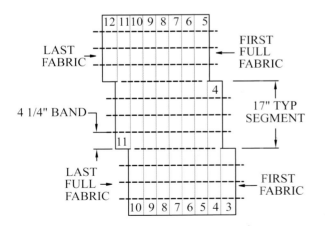

Cut each 17" segment into four 4¼" bands
Reassemble one band from each segment into blocks A1–A4

Diagram 5, 4¼ inches.

Strips for Blocks A1–A4

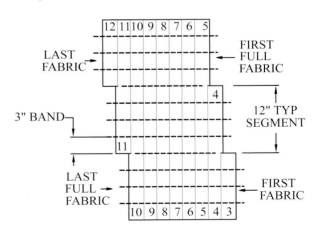

Cut each 12" segment into four 3" bands
Reassemble one band from each segment into blocks A1–A4

Diagram 5, Small.

FABRIC BANDS						
GROUP	A	B	C	D	E	F*
FIRST FABRIC	3	8	13	18	23	28
FIRST FULL 40" FABRIC	7	12	17	22	27	30
LAST FULL 40" FABRIC	27	32	37	42	47	52
LAST FABRIC	31	36	41	46	51	54

*24" wide group: three bands
All groups A through E have five bands of 8" sections
Group F has three bands of 8" sections

Diagram 6, Large.

FABRIC COLORS				
GROUP	A	B	C	D
FIRST 17" LONG FABRIC STRIP	3	6	9	12
FIRST 51" LONG (34" GROUP D) FABRIC STRIP	5	8	11	13
LAST 51" LONG (34" GROUP D) FABRIC STRIP	10	13	16	19
LAST 17" LONG FABRIC STRIP	12	15	18	20

Groups A, B & C have three 17" segments
Group D has two 17" segments

Diagram 6, 4¼ inches.

FABRIC BANDS					
GROUP	A	B	C	D	E*
FIRST FABRIC	3	8	13	18	23
FIRST FULL 40" FABRIC	7	12	17	22	26
LAST FULL 40" FABRIC	22	27	32	37	42
LAST FABRIC	26	31	36	41	45

*32" wide group: four bands
All groups A through D have five bands of 8" sections
Group E has four bands of 8" sections

Diagram 6, Medium.

FABRIC COLORS				
GROUP	A	B	C	D
FIRST 12" LONG FABRIC STRIP	3	6	9	12
FIRST 36" LONG (24" GROUP D) FABRIC STRIP	5	8	11	13
LAST 36" LONG (24" GROUP D) FABRIC STRIP	10	13	16	19
LAST 12" LONG FABRIC STRIP	12	15	18	20

Groups A, B & C have three 12" segments
Group D has two 12" segments

Diagram 6, Small.

Seam Pressing Instructions

Each group is a set of 5 pieced together 4 times
Press seam allowances in alternate directions
for each band starting from the center

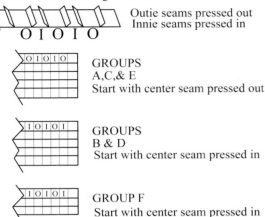

Outie seams pressed out
Innie seams pressed in

GROUPS
A, C, & E
Start with center seam pressed out

GROUPS
B & D
Start with center seam pressed in

GROUP F
Start with center seam pressed in

Diagram 7, Large.

Seam Pressing Instructions

Each group is a set of
9 or 10 strips pieced together
Press seam allowances in
alternate directions for each
band starting from the center

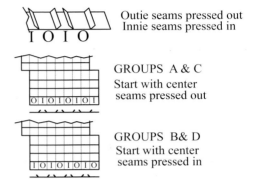

Outie seams pressed out
Innie seams pressed in

GROUPS A & C
Start with center
seams pressed out

GROUPS B & D
Start with center
seams pressed in

Diagram 7, 4¼ inches.

Seam Pressing Instructions

Each group is a set of 5 pieced together 4 times
Press seam allowances in alternate directions
for each band starting from the center

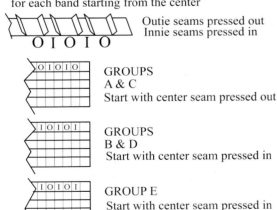

Outie seams pressed out
Innie seams pressed in

GROUPS
A & C
Start with center seam pressed out

GROUPS
B & D
Start with center seam pressed in

GROUP E
Start with center seam pressed in

Diagram 7, Medium.

Seam Pressing Instructions

Each group is a set of
9 or 10 strips pieced together
Press seam allowances in
alternate directions for each
band starting from the center

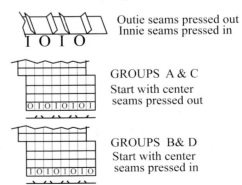

Outie seams pressed out
Innie seams pressed in

GROUPS A & C
Start with center
seams pressed out

GROUPS B & D
Start with center
seams pressed in

Diagram 7, Small.

Follow the Fabric Bands charts in Diagram 6 for each of the Groups A through F. All strips have five bands of 8" sections, and a 2" cut for each of the A sections, except the F Group, which has three bands of 8" sections.

When the A band is sewn and pressed, go to the B band (Diagram 6), referring to the first fabric #8, and continue adding strips until coming to the first full 40" cut. Always sew from right to left starting at one end. Remember when adding the staggered strips on the opposite side to start sewing at the top.

Another tip: When sewing long lengths, either use an even feed foot on the machine or gently tug on the underneath fabric.

Go to the #3, first fabric in your magazine layout, then # 4 and #5 and so on, always referring to the fabric swatch and stitching right to left. The four first and last strips are staggered with 21 long 40" strips in the middle. Recheck that all of the 40" cuts are exact, especially as you add #28 for the A Group, #33 for the B Group, #38 for the C Group, #43 for the D Group, #48 for the E Group, and #53 for the F Group.

Pressing becomes important once all strips are sewn. The A, C, and E groups all start with the center seam pressed out. The B, D, and F groups start with the center seam pressed in.

Once the A bands are sewn, continue with each of the other bands. Each time the first fabric, last fabric, is indicated, along with the full 40" cut strip. With these groups all sewn together it becomes obvious that this is a four-bobbin pieced quilt. Everyone works in different ways, so sewing each band together is one way, with an alternate method being to start cutting apart the A band into the 8" segments—five times—and eventually into the sewn segments placed on your design wall next to the connectors.

The following sewn strips correspond to Diagram 5 from A band through F band. Follow Diagram 6 (Large) indicating each band, with F having only three 8" sections. (Note that on band E, the #23 fabric strip needed to be pressed back.)

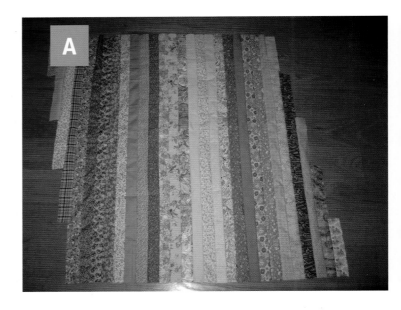

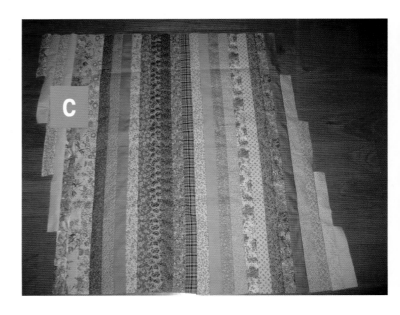

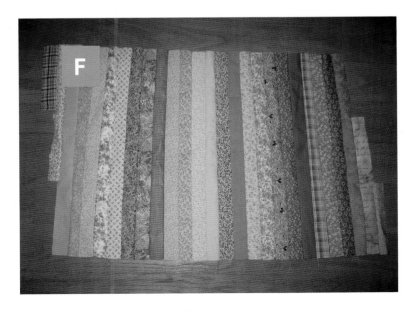

FOURTH STEP: CUTTING AND RE-PIECING

Starting with Group A, which has been stitched and pressed, cut this apart every 8", then into 4" segments and eventually the 2" rows. Take a cut strip from each of the five sections, in order, and pin together. Use a large 12" square ruler and other long rulers to aid in this process. These are then sewn together in order. Five rows stack in order, while the other five rows stack in a reverse order for the mirror image. Note how the seams automatically stagger in order to release and twirl the seam allowances. Press the back along with the front side. Place these four A sections on the design set up next to the connectors. Complete B, C, D, E, and F.

As you progress with the pressing, now is the time to twirl each intersection. This allows for a balanced soft intersection and becomes a rather obsessive maneuver, setting your quilt apart!

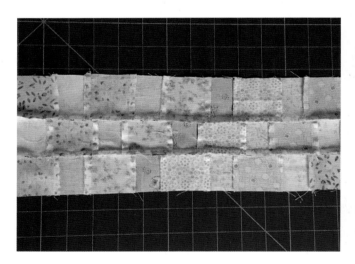

Closed seams are sewn staggered across the rows with the "innies" (seams pressed inward) and the "outies" (seams pressed outward).

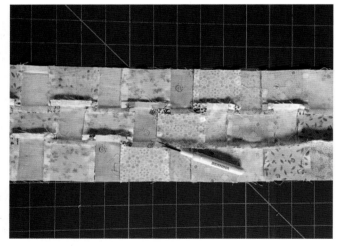

Use a seam ripper or a pin to release stitches beyond the connecting row seams. Then twirl the intersection and press. Note that the seams alternate, going clockwise then counterclockwise.

Refer to the B and C connectors as you pin. Two sets are reversed.

After completing each section, sew the connectors including #1 square either vertically or horizontally. That will determine how remaining sections are attached for the completed quilt.

BACKING FABRIC:
5 yards

BINDING REQUIREMENTS:
9 yards of 2¼" wide cut fabric.

Take one strip from each of the five 8" cuts (cut into 2" widths) and pin those for future sewing together.

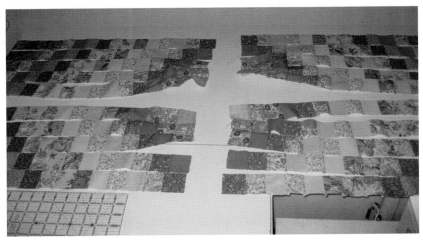

Midnight

Medium Version of The Real Trip Around the World
58½" × 70½"
(with 2" side border and 7" top and bottom border:
60½" × 84½")

What fun to sort out my stash and gather all of the blacks, grays, and a few bright fabrics for this Real Trip Around the World quilt called Midnight. Once again all of the vertical cuts are 2", but fewer numbers, stopping at 45 different cuts.

Georgia's College Quilt

63¾" × 86¼"
(9" borders: 72¾" × 95¼")

For this college-bound granddaughter I chose more-sophisticated conversation prints combined with black fabric. All the even numbers were cut with the solid color versus the prints. This time the standard width to cut is 4¼" and when sewn, 3¾". With only 20 fabrics, this goes even faster than the smaller quilt.

BINDING REQUIREMENTS:
8 yards of binding cut 2¼" wide.

The Trip Around the Ranch Quilt

42½" × 57½"

Gathering all of my western fabric, from horses to fishing to cowboy boots, made for a fun quilt. Here the cuts are 3" wide and, when sewn, 2½".

The actual quilt is narrower than the cutting instructions. I felt the length required more width; hence an extra row on each side was added.

Squares & Triangles: Waste Not Want Not Quilt

70" × 90"

This is a true scrappy star quilt. The play of light and dark small prints in each block and border gives it a subtle special character. The more the merrier makes this quilt work and gives it the beautiful patina. Make it as Audrey made it; one block at a time and then lap quilt it in sections.

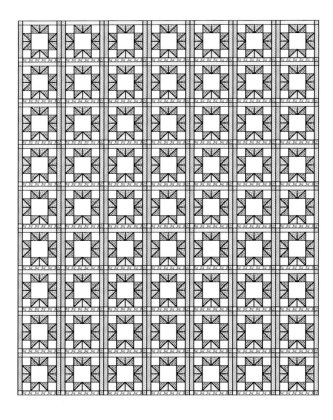

By Audrey Tews, a former student.

Cutting:

For one block (make 63 blocks):

One center print 4½" square.

Four corner prints 2½" square.

Two contrasting prints for half-square triangles 6" square.

Rectangles for borders; 4 cut 1½" × 8½".

Corner squares; 4 cut 1½" square.

Method:

With right sides together of the 6" squares, sew on either side of each diagonal line. Cut apart in quarter sections plus each diagonal. See diagram.

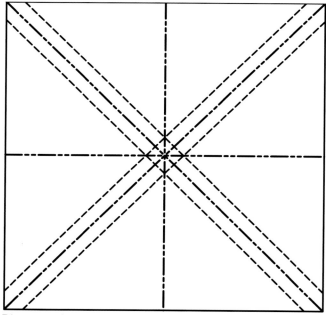

Diagram of the half-square triangles made from the 6" squares.

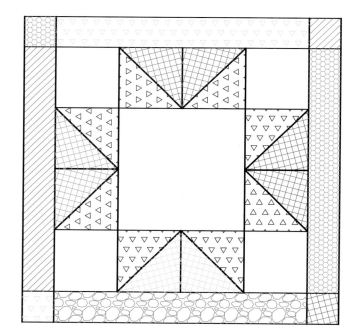

Open each half-square triangle, then press and trim to eight 2½" squares. Sew half-square triangles together four times to create four rectangles; take caution not to turn triangles the wrong way. Sew four sets of half-square triangles together to create four rectangles.

Sew corner prints to two sets of rectangles. Press connecting seams outward.

Sew the side rectangles to the center square. Press seams inward. Sew the top and bottom rectangles to complete the 8½" square, staggering seams.

Add side borders; sew four small squares to the ends of top and bottom borders and complete block. This block should measure 10½" square.

BINDING REQUIREMENTS:
9 yards of 2¼" wide cut fabric.

This quilt was hand quilted in two sections, making it easier to handle and complete. One section had four rows and another had five rows, each section having seven blocks across.

The center square and borders are cross-hatched quilted, while the remainder has ¼" quilting from the pieced areas. This quilt received judge's choice and a first-prize award in the annual Harvest of Quilts Show in Hendersonville, North Carolina.

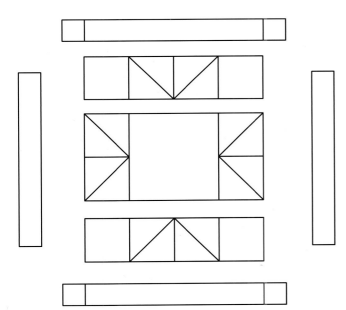

Log Cabin Revisited Quilt

82" × 91½"

For all its simplicity the Log Cabin quilt has so many setting options that it is always worthy of a remake. This quilt's uniqueness is the addition of denim strips along with varying widths of the log additions. Once the 72 blocks (9½" square) are complete, the setting is optional. So many to choose from makes you just want to make more than one quilt.

Yes, just adding strips cut a certain width to a center bright square (always thought of as the fire in the cabin)

is possible, but to get it right, with just a bit more effort, cutting out specific-length strips will ensure a perfect block. Often, when just adding strips, the cross-grain cuts have more give and will end up distorting the initial square.

Scraps: The more varied the scraps, the more exciting. Note that the adjacent different scraps are the same in each block. Choose the lightest-weight denim as you separate the lights and the darks.

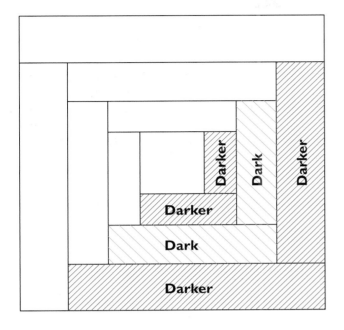

Dark block schematic.

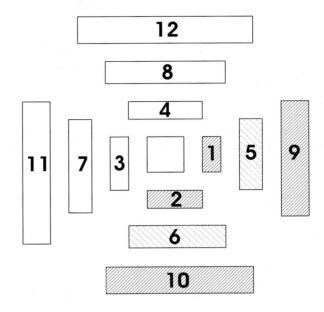

Dark block piecing sequence.

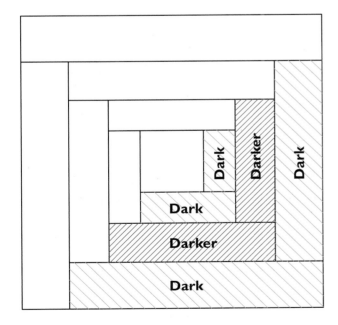

Light block schematic.

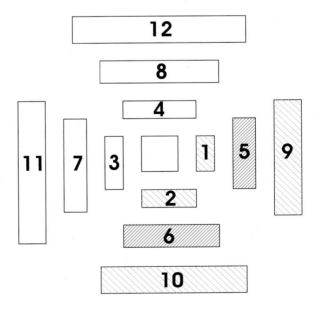

Light block piecing sequence.

Cutting:

Dark strips (36 of each)
    $1\frac{1}{2}$" × $2\frac{1}{2}$"
    $1\frac{1}{2}$" × $3\frac{1}{2}$"
    $1\frac{3}{4}$" × $4\frac{1}{2}$"
    $1\frac{3}{4}$" × $5\frac{3}{4}$"
    2" × 7"
    2" × $8\frac{1}{2}$"

Darker strips (36 of each)
    $1\frac{1}{2}$" × $2\frac{1}{2}$"
    $1\frac{1}{2}$" × $3\frac{1}{2}$"
    $1\frac{3}{4}$" × $4\frac{1}{2}$"
    $1\frac{3}{4}$" × $5\frac{3}{4}$"
    2" × 7"
    2" × $8\frac{1}{2}$"

Light printed scraps
(72 of each)

Cut 72 accent $2\frac{1}{2}$" squares

    $1\frac{1}{2}$" × $3\frac{1}{2}$" × $1\frac{1}{2}$" × $4\frac{1}{2}$" same fabric
    $1\frac{3}{4}$" × $5\frac{3}{4}$" × $1\frac{3}{4}$" × 7" same fabric
    2" × $8\frac{1}{2}$" × 2" × 10" same fabric

Cut 2 side borders 86" × $3\frac{1}{2}$"
Cut 2 top and bottom borders $82\frac{1}{2}$" × $3\frac{1}{2}$"

Method:

To make the first 36 blocks, start out stitching from the center square with dark strips added in a clockwise manner. After two logs (strips) are added, pick up the next two light logs to be added. Then switch to the next two darker logs. Continue adding logs in a clockwise manner until all 12 logs are added. Then, to make the second 36 blocks, start out stitching from the center square with the darker strips added clockwise. Follow the same system of clockwise addition. This avoids the double-dark connection when blocks are sewn together. Trim each of the 72 blocks to a 10" square.

Streak of Lightning.

Arrange the 72 blocks in the desired setting. Can you find the chosen setting? It is Streak of Lightning, but there are eleven other choices. Each of the nine horizontal rows, giving added length for pillow coverage, has eight blocks to be stitched together.

A 3" border was added. The side borders were added first, then the top and bottom borders.

Hint: Continuous sewing of each strip addition saves time, since there is no trimming with exact cuts planned ahead.

I quilted this entire quilt on my Bernina Artista 170 sewing machine.

BINDING REQUIREMENTS:
10 yards of 2¼" wide cut fabric.

Barn Raising.

Around the Logs.

Center Star.

Face Up.

Square Off.

Right On.

Zeros and X's.

Straight Furrows.

Triangle Mirror Image.

This 'n' That.

Up and Down.

Squares & Rectangles: Scrap Soup Quilt

82" × 102"

Quilted by Nancy Clayburn

This is a clean-up-the-stash quilt devoid of half-square triangles, quarter-square triangles, narrow points, or intricate appliqué. It is an opportunity to play with your color scraps, swap, and even reminisce. Working with a group of like-minded quilters adds to the stash opportunities. The Scrap Soup design has two other sizes, small and wall-hanging size—plus a miniature doll bed size. Have fun varying the background or keeping the diamond shape light, bright, or dark. The options here are endless!

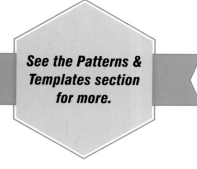

See the Patterns & Templates section for more.

Supplies:

Background Fabric: 4½ yards (I used navy and black scraps, but printed muslin is a favorite)

Top and Bottom Accent Border: 1 yard (any contrast that accents background choice)

Scraps: 70 strips × 2½" wide and 30" long or as many as people will spare. (Describing their origin or previous use is a fun scrap-sharing idea.)

Flannel or full-size batting design wall

Cutting:

Background Fabric: Light	Border (top and bottom & sides)
50 rectangles 8½" × 2½"	12 rectangles 8½" × 2½"
20 rectangles 10½" × 2½"	84 rectangles 4½" × 2½"
140 rectangles 4½" × 2½"	22 squares 2½" × 2½"
122 rectangles 6½" × 2½"	12 rectangles 6½" × 2½"
163 squares 2½" × 2½"	

Method:

1. Mount full-size batting or flannel sheet on a visible wall.

2. Start with the middle section, A, arranging the seven rows by positioning the background fabrics. There will be five of these A sections, with connector rows, B, in between and on the sides. Leave space for the scrap fabric. With chosen border accents, top and bottom fabrics, position those in place along with each A section. Keep the schematic close at hand to guide in the proper lengths of each fabric cut.

3. The blue-shaded areas in the large quilt schematic represent the different scrap blocks. In each A section there are seven blocks plus part of six blocks. The beauty of this quilt is that the blocks are automatically pieced into the rows. Start cutting the scraps apart in the following sets for each block within the A rows; 4½" — 4½" — 6½" — 6½" — 2½" — 2½", which makes up one scrap block.

4. With the seven rows laid out, pin the strips together. Piece each row, starting at one end, then pick up the opposite end in the kite system.

   Start with with the center row of each seven segments. As you line up the next row to stitch, the previous seam line becomes a guide to keep cross seams lined up properly. Continue this set up for the remaining four segments. Note the outside border selections for the A segments.

   Pressing tips: Press all closed seams in the same direction.

5. Lay out and position the B connector rows. The two outside rows contain border cuts and background fabric cuts.

6. Connect all A vertical sections with the B connector rows. The border is built in as the row connection is sewn.

BINDING REQUIREMENTS:
Yes, I used a variety of leftover scraps sewn together with bias connections for the binding. It took 10½ yards cut 2¼" wide.

Class results at John C. Campbell Folk School.

Medium Scrap Soup

31" × 33"

Reduce the width of all cuts to 1½". Keep the same format of A sections with seven rows (three A sections) and four B connector strips.

Here the contrast is scrap fabric for the background, whereas light becomes the block area and the top and bottom wave.

Cutting:

All widths are 1½".

Scraps, A Section	Scraps, B Section
Cut 27 = 1½"	Cut 20 = 1½"
Cut 36 = 2½"	Cut 8 = 3½"
Cut 18 = 3½"	
Cut 12 = 5½"	
Cut 30 = 4½"	

Blocks and Top and Bottom Wave

Light, A Section	B Section
Cut 36 = 1½"	Cut 16 = 2½"
Cut 54 = 2½"	Cut 8 = 4½"
Cut 30 = 3½"	

The method of construction is the same with the addition of a 3" border.

Cut 2 top and bottom borders 3½" × 25½", and stitch in place.

Cut 2 side borders 3½" × 27½", and stitch in place to complete.

See the Patterns & Templates section for more.

Miniature Scrap Soup

16½" × 21"

Reduce the width of all cuts to 1". Keep the same format of A sections with seven rows (three of these) and four B connector strips.

Here the blocks plus the top and bottom wave use scrap fabrics, and the background is light.

Cutting:

Scraps, A Section
Cut 36 = 1"
Cut 54 = 1½"
Cut 30 = 2"

Scraps, B Section
Cut 16 = 1½"
Cut 8 = 2½"

Light or Background A Section
Cut 27 = 1"
Cut 36 = 1½"
Cut 18 = 2"
Cut 30 = 2½"
Cut 12 = 3"

B Section
Cut 20 = 1"
Cut 8 = 2"

First end border on top and bottom:
Cut 4 lights 2" × 1½"   Cut 4 lights 3" × 1½"
Cut 6 scraps 2" × 1½"

Second/outside border top and bottom:
Cut 4 lights 2½" × 1½"   Cut 4 lights 4" × 1½"
Cut 6 scraps 1" × 1½"

A 2" border in polka dots:
Cut 2 borders: 2½" × 17½" for the top and bottom
Cut 2 borders: 2½" × 17½" for the sides

Finishing: Once the quilt was pieced and bordered, I tacked the centers of each scrap block with tiny pearl buttons and simply hand quilted in the ditch at each long end.

It has become a charming, sweet cover-up on the family iron doll bed, complete with a collection of china dolls peeking out from under the coverlet.

See the Patterns & Templates section for more.

Triangles: Hall of Fame Autograph Quilt

80¾" × 80¾"

Quilted by Kathy Boxell, member of Marie Webster Quilt Guild and former board president

A brief history of this quilt: In 2007 I began this signature quilt to raise money for the Quilters Hall of Fame in Marion, Indiana (www.quiltershalloffame.net). Some blocks were made at Celebration in a machine competition between a treadle machine and my Bernina. What fun to watch Eleanor Burns and myself pedal and stitch. The quilt and the accompanying sham were completed for the 2011 Celebration. It was purchased by Ralph and Janis James and donated to the collection of the Quilters Hall of Fame. Over 144 signatures that also include the pillow shams make this a meaningful and lasting legacy.

Honoree signatures include Virginia Avery, Sheila Betterton, Jinny Beyer, Georgia Bonesteel, Barbara Brackman, Karey Patterson Bresenhan, Eleanor Burns, Nancy Crow, Jeffrey Gutcheon, Jonathan Holstein, Michael James, Helen Kelley, Bonnie Leman, Yvonne Porcella, and Bets Ramsey.

A light diagonal signature strip is flanked by four bright prints. When set together between the fabric scrap prints, the autographs form a lattice of pinwheels. Looking closer, one can spot repeat prints. So, two prints go twice as far, with a quick stitching and cutting method.

Cutting:

Assemble 72 pairs of 6" square cut scraps; each pair makes two 6½" square (6" sewn) blocks.

Cut four light inner borders 2½ " × 76½"

Cut 132 triangles for the outer scrap border, using template A. Speed cutting: cut 33 squares 6" on the diagonal both ways.

Cut 144 light template B for autographs. Freezer paper pressed on the backside stabilizes the fabric. Optional cut would be strips cut 2¼" wide and 9¼" long with 45-degree angle at each end. Note that the ends will be on the bias. Use a permanent marker, tested, for the signatures.

Method:

With a pair of 6" print fabrics, right sides together, draw a diagonal line from corner to corner. Stitch a ¼" seam on either side of this line. Cut apart on drawn line and the adjacent diagonal. Mix and match the pieced triangles with a B signature template in between. Assemble all 72 pairs, then mark and sew in a continuous kite fashion on one side and the next side.

Assemble the quilt in rows with 12 blocks across and 12 blocks down. The 6" blocks can be sewn into four patches for ease in assembly. Play with a balance of color and prints along with the best position of autographs.

Sew the light borders on all four sides with mitered borders.

Stitch the 33 triangles for each side of the square quilt.

BINDING REQUIREMENTS:
9 yards of 2¼" wide cut fabric.

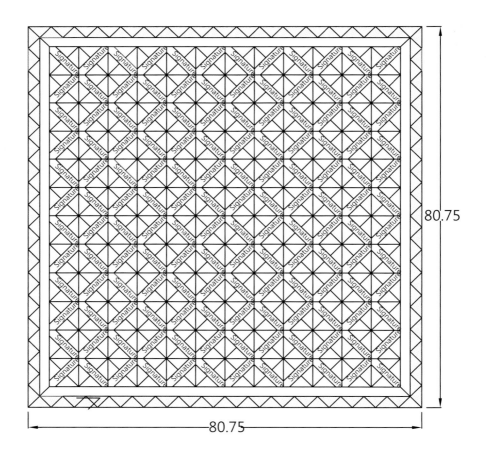

80.75

80.75

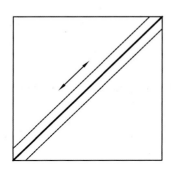

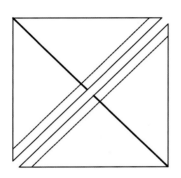

See the Patterns & Templates section for more.

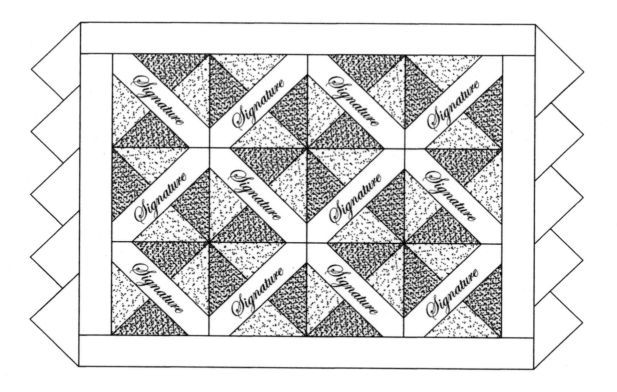

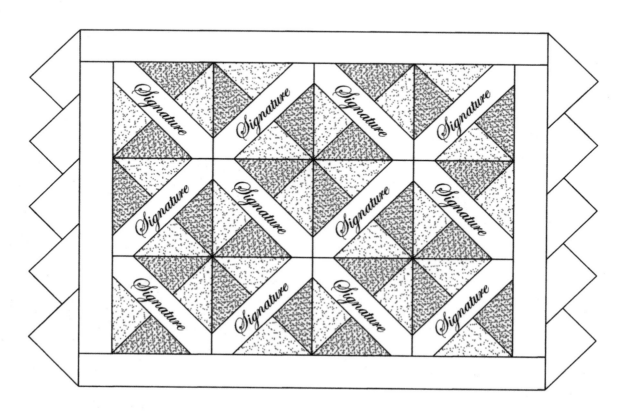

Pillow Shams

For the sham, assemble 12 pairs of scrap 6" squares. Draw a diagonal line, stitch on either side, cut apart, and cut apart on the other diagonal. Mix and match these triangles with a signature in between for 24 squares, 6½".

Stitch three rows of four blocks for each of the shams. The size: 24" × 18" plus seam allowances for each sham.

Cut four light borders for each: 2½" × 18½" for the sides. Cut four light borders for the top and bottom: 2½" × 24½".

Cut two sham backings, one for each sham, 22½" × 24½". Stitch each of these rectangles to a long edge of the sham.

Prepare prairie points for each side end for the shams. Cut 20 scrap squares 6", fold on the diagonal, fold again, and with the open edge overlap the angled corner onto the next folded point. Pin together to fit the 22" span. Machine stitch five prairie points onto each end, with the right angles directed inward and the raw edges aligned. Machine baste in place.

Cut a lining for the sham 44½" × 28½". With the right sides together, stitch the side seams. Hint: Stitch with the lining against feed dogs, making it possible to see the machine basting stitches. Turn inside out, then top stitch each side four times.

Sew the front and the backing together, continuing into the lining, leaving about a 10" opening to whip stitch closed. Press the sides. A pillow can slip in either side to match the quilt.

Equilateral Triangles: Cane Cousin Quilt

74¾" × 92"

Have you ever caned a chair? Years ago I did just that, never guessing I'd name a quilt a relative of the process of caning. In fact, my rocking chair might have been used by Lottie Sayler, my great-grandmother, when she pieced the Job's Troubles quilt top around 1898.

The Cane Cousin is a great chance to focus on the center hexagon for fussy-cut strips, plaids, or a favorite floral print. This quilt has all of the patchwork elements that I have grown to enjoy piecing and teaching students: mathematical cutting sans templates, twirled intersections, dog ear accumulation, and patience. Templates are included, but quick cutting is shown.

Supplies:

Stripe fabric: 2½ yards (each stripe hexagon, 5" × 19")

Hexagon fabric: 1¾ yards

Dark (DK), Bright (BR), and Light (LT) fabric: 1¾ yards each

12 large border triangles: ½ yard

Inside border: ¾ yard

Outside Pieced Border: Scraps of stripe fabric; 1 yard of background fabric

Cutting:

Using template A, "fussy" cut* 6 triangles for each of the 36 hexagons. Six of the hexagons will form 12 half hexagons to be sewn on the sides. Another option is using the D template and cutting 30 print hexagons and 12 half hexagons (include seam allowance on the long side).

B template: Cut 68 dark fabrics, 68 bright fabrics, and 68 light fabrics. Cut a fabric strip 2⅛" wide, selvage to selvage on the crosswise, 10 times of each color. You can stack the three different colors for quick cutting. Using the 60-degree angle on a ruler, cut seven trapezoids out of each row, with a distance of 6⅝" between each wide angle. Save eight of each color for the side half hexagons. Hint: Use the first cut template as a repeat cut pattern.

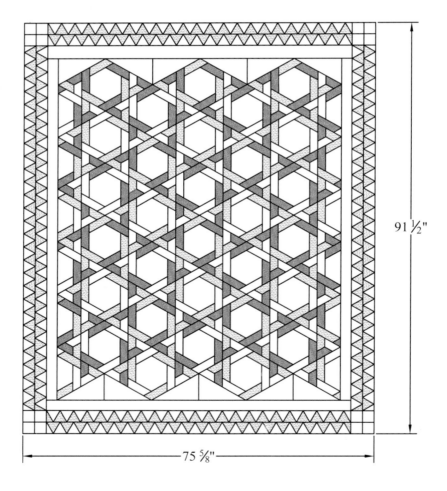

91 ½"

75 ⅝"

*Fussy cutting means positioning the A template the same way each time for the strips to form a continuous circle.

C template: Cut 72 dark fabrics, 72 bright fabrics, and 72 light fabrics. Cut a fabric strip 2⅛" wide, selvage to selvage on the crosswise, seven times for each color. Using the 60-degree angle on a ruler, cut 11 templates out of each row, with a distance of 4¾" between wide angles. Save 12 or six sets of each for the side half hexagons. Hint: Use the first cut template as a repeat cut pattern.

Border Half Diamonds

B++ figure and figure B+: Cut 4 DK, 4 BR, and 4 LT of each figures.

Use the templates given to cut out these side sets in half diamonds.

Setting Triangle

F Triangle figure: Cut six sets of mirror images

Border

Side borders: Cut two strips 2⅞" × 76¾".

Top and bottom border: Cut two strips 3⅜" × 65¼".

Pieced rickrack outside border (finished width = 5").

Template E to form rickrack accents, cutting stripe and background fabric.

Template E: Inner side border; cut 56 background fabrics, then cut 54 stripe fabric plus four half E template (add seam allowances).

Template E: Outer side border; cut 56 stripe fabric, then *cut 54 background plus half E (add seam allowances).

Template E: Top and bottom inner border; *Cut 44 E plus two half E background, then cut 44 E stripe plus two half E (add seam allowance).

Template E: Top and bottom outer border; *Cut 44 E background. Cut 44 stripe fabric plus two half E template (add seam allowance).

Corners

Four patches made from various prints. Cut 16 squares 3" and stitch into four patches = 5½" (5" squares finished).

* Quick cutting for the background E triangles:
Cut 10 rows of inner background fabric 3¼" wide (selvage to selvage on the crosswise). Cut 9 rows of a different outer background color 3¼" wide. With the 60-degree angle on ruler cut 200 inner E triangles and 186 outer E triangle background. Use the template E, adding a ¼" seam allowance on the right angle side for any partial end pieces.

* Quick cutting for the stripe E triangles:
Cut a mixture of 20 different stripe fabrics 3¼" wide to yield 396 Es. Use the template E, adding a ¼" seam allowance on the right angle side for any partial end pieces. Cuts are based on yielding 19 E fabric triangles from each row.

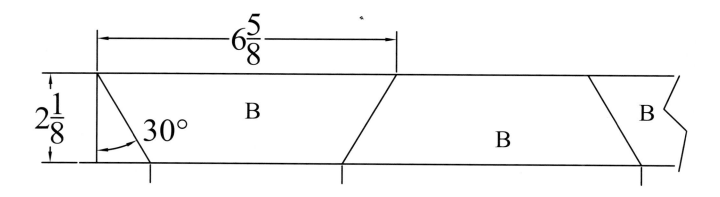

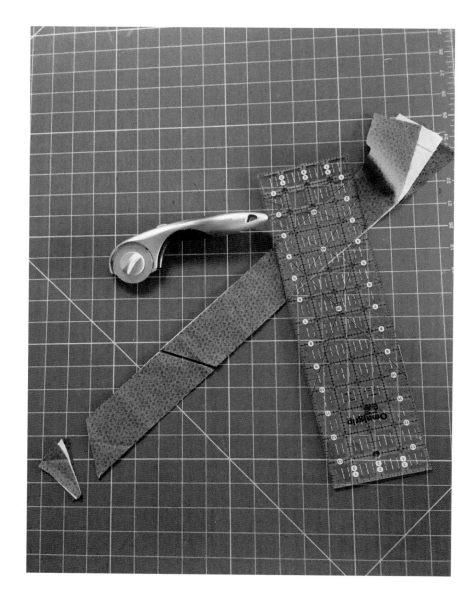

Quick cutting for B.

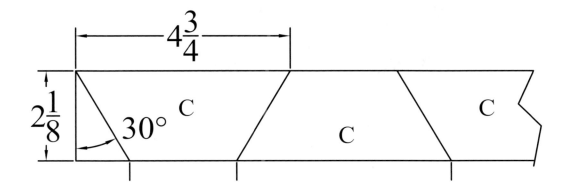

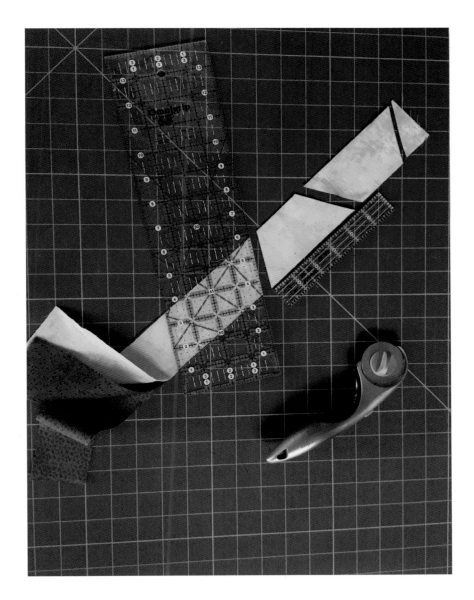

Quick cutting for C.

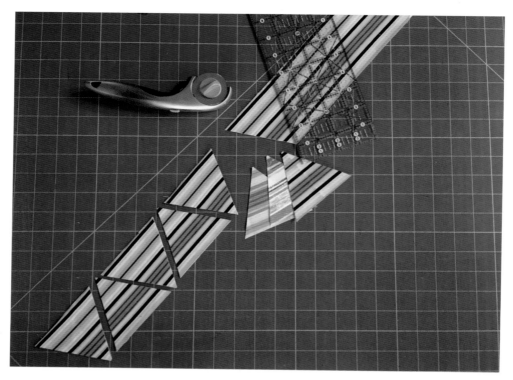

Quick cutting for E, stripe fabric.

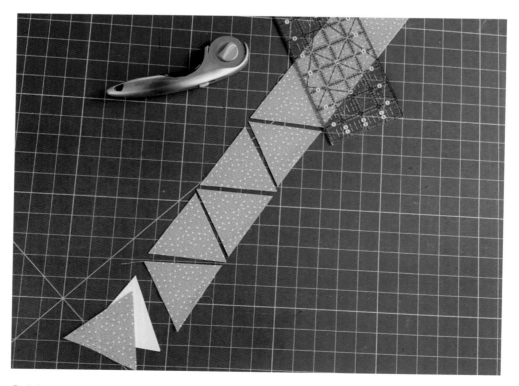

Quick cutting for E, two background fabrics.

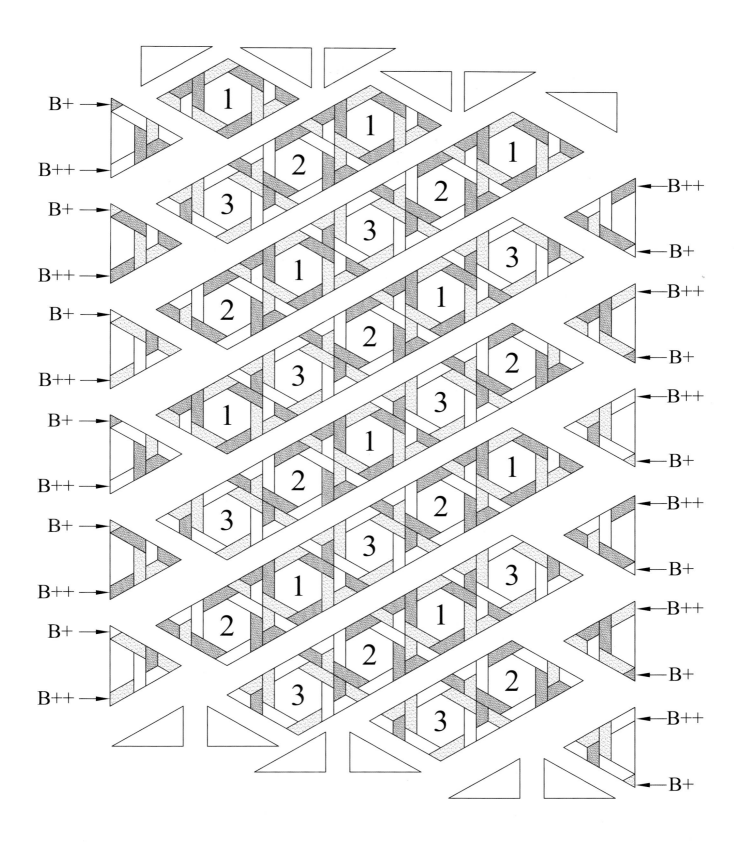

Method:

1. Using the A templates that are cut out, sew 30 hexagons and 12 half hexagons together, using variously striped fabric.

   Sew in twos, press seam allowance in same direction, set in last set, always stopping at inside ¼", trim "dog ears," and twirl intersection for a flat connection.

2. Make 30 hexagons and 12 half hexagons, using three different settings of the same DK, BR, and LT fabrics. Note #1, #2, and #3 diamond schematics, sewing 10 diamonds each with a different addition of the B template. The side half hexagons use four different additions of the B template. Follow the schematic as a stitching guide.

   Stitch 30 D hexagons together. Stitch 12 D half hexagons together. Piece two sets of triangle, A, together. Finger press seams in the same direction, closed seams. Add extra triangle to each side, with seams finger pressed again in the same direction. Match centers, stitch, and then twirl center intersection. (I tried two other methods but found this to be better for less bulk and flat centers.)

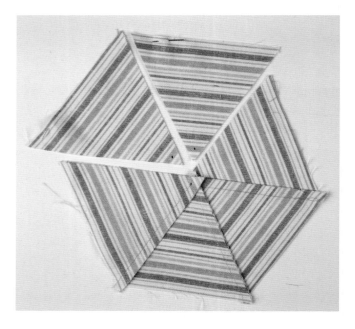

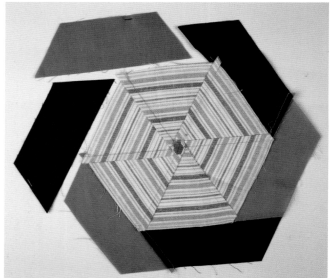

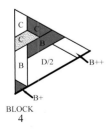

BLOCK
4

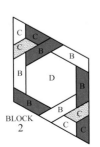

BLOCK
2

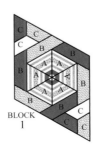

BLOCK
1

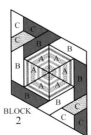

BLOCK
2

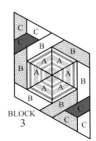

BLOCK
3

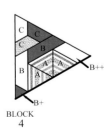

BLOCK
4

For B addition, stitch backwards, out to the ¼" the first time, where there is an extension. Add remaining B figures in a counter-clockwise manner. Add the last B figure and compete sewing the short extension.

3. Sew the C sets together 42 times, 30 for large diamonds and 12 for the side half hexagons. Sew up to the ¼" center seam; back stitch for ease in creating a floating seam allowance. Note how this pieced C triangle matches the B trapezoid forming the diamond. Sew these C sets to opposite end of the completed hexagons, identifying each of the four blocks.

Refer to the explosion diagram for positioning diamonds in a diagonal setting for piecing the rows together. Label the #1, #2, and #3 diamonds for ease in proper placement. Add the F triangle setting template.

Sew the side borders to the top; add the top and bottom borders.

With border E fabrics cut out, sew the eight rows of triangles together, balancing the print fabrics in place. Sew the top and bottom borders first, then adding the side borders and the corner four patches.

I am proud to say I quilted this entirely on my Bernina sewing machine, using several decorative stitches.

BINDING REQUIREMENTS:
9½ yards of 2¼" wide cut fabric.

Diamonds: Lone Star King Size Quilt

104½" × 104½" (point to point star: 72½")

It should be a rite of passage: every quilter must make a Lone Star quilt. The repetition of color in this dynamic star adds beauty to any bed, wall, or even a table skirt. Years ago it was something I only admired, until the rotary cutter, strata stitching, and simple math evolved.

Whenever I pull out a calculator in class to teach quilt math, I make sure to lock the classroom doors first.

For sure, when I taught quilt math on television, I could feel people fading away. But once you find the benefit of using the decimal system for cutting fabric, you will be forever grateful. The formula for any size of Lone Star quilt is amazing and so simple.

First: determine the size you want, point to point, for your quilt.

Second: divide that amount by 4.8.

Third: take that amount and divide that by the number of diamonds across one row.

Fourth: that amount is the width of the finished diamond star.

Fifth: add 0.5 or ½" to that width to give you the cuts for the strata.

The formula for star speed piecing has been perfected in Barbara Johannah's *Crystal Piecing* book and Jean Affleck and Pat Cairns's book *Contemporary Quilting Techniques: A Modular Approach.*

An array of blues and yellow diamonds are surrounded by toile accents. It pleases the eye in our blue-painted bedroom.

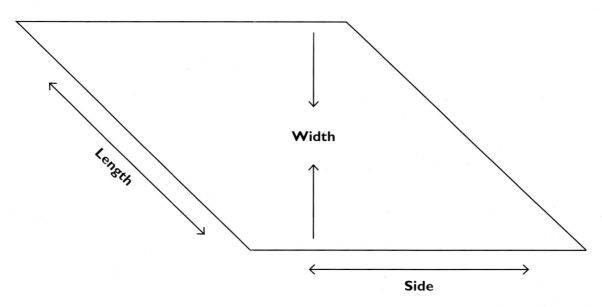

45-degree diamond.

Supplies and Cutting:

Choose a selection of five coordinated fabrics, ½ yard for each color.

> Cut a square 22½", then cut apart on both diagonals for the setting outside triangle. Cut two squares (toile) 22⅛", then cut apart on the diagonal. Cut two squares 22⅛", then cut apart on the diagonal for corner triangles.

Border:

> Cut four border strips 2½" × 73"; cut two border strips 5½" × 73"; cut two border strips 7½" × 73".

> Cut four long, vertical strips 2½" × 105"; cut two vertical strips 5" × 105"; cut two vertical strips 7½" × 105".

Method:

Cut five strips 3½" wide with each of the five chosen fabrics, selvage to selvage. Label the colors #1 through #5. Stack the eight strips, starting with #1 through #5. Now stack the five fabrics in groups to stitch, #1 through #5 (Group A), then #2 through #5 and #1 (Group B), then #3 through #2 (Group C), and so forth.

Sew these bands together, starting with #1 through #5, staggering the right angle of each 3" before starting each new color. Sew the next stratum starting with #2 color. After #5, start again with #1 color. The opposite end will be staggered also. Press with all closed seams to form "innies" and "outies" that alternate for each group. This step results in five pieced strata.

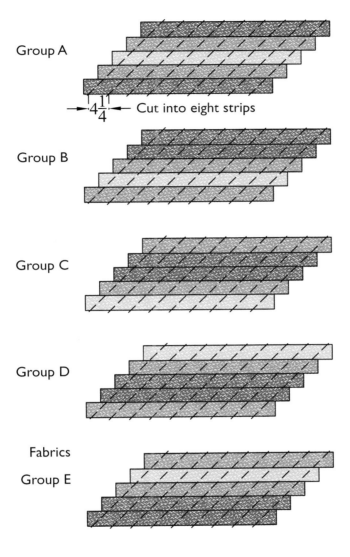

Group A

$4\frac{1}{4}$ — Cut into eight strips

Group B

Group C

Group D

Fabrics

Group E

With a ruler in place, align the 45-degree mark at one end of the strata. Cut each stratum every 3½" to yield eight strips, one for each point of the star.

Hint: With masking tape, mark the 45-degree angle along with 3½" width.

To form the eight star points, sew a progressive strip starting at A, then B, C, D, and E. "Pin and peek" so that intersections align. These intersections can be twirled once a few stitches are released.

Once pressed, the star can be stitched together. Sew in sets of two diamonds. At the outside right angle, sew only up to the ¼", then stop and back stitch. Sew in halves. Press connecting diamonds seams in the same direction. Pin center intersection so seams are staggered. Complete center seam and then create twirl of center intersection by releasing stitches from raw edges to the center seam.

Sew the outside setting triangles into place four times. Align the 45-degree angles and sew up to the ¼"; backstitch to secure. The corner squares can be sewn in by aligning the right angles and sewing up to the inside ¼" seam and back stitching.

Complete with pieced border accents top and bottom. Finish with the side pieced borders. Due to the king size, I curved the corners.

Binding Requirements: 12 yards of 2 ¼" wide cut fabric.

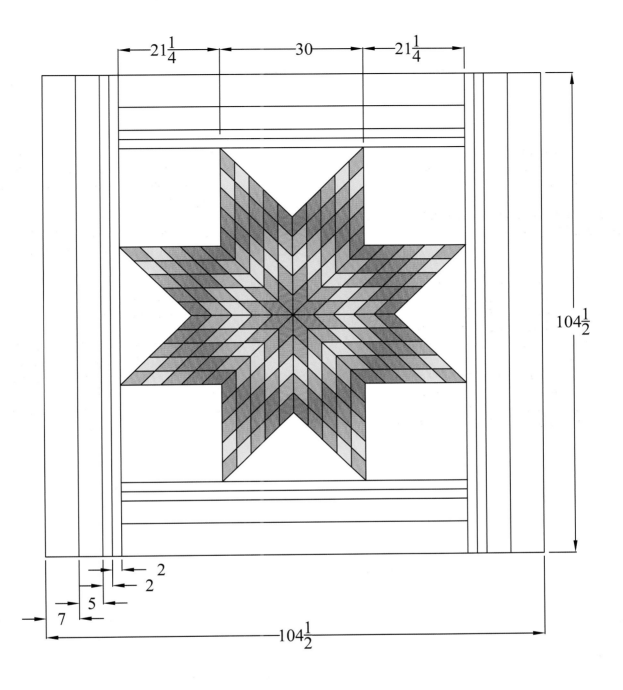

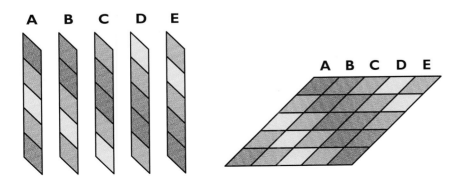

Lone Star Table Skirt

72" round patchwork table skirt

The same principle and method for the Lone Star quilt applies here.

Supplies:

Choose a selection of six coordinated fabrics with ½ yard of each color.

Choose setting fabric that frames star; 1½ yards plus cut 16 accent strips 2" × 21".

Method:

Cut six strips 3" wide with the six chosen fabrics. Label the colors #1 through #6. Stack the six strips, starting with #1 through #6, and pin together. Follow the same method above to create the eight pieced stars. The outside edge of the pieced star is 21". Stitch the accent strips to either side of star points; stop at ¼" seam allowance, then back stitch in place, as in a mitered corner, to complete the extended seam.

To determine the size of the set in curved square (right angle on one side with opposite curved area), use a string attached to a pencil, with the radius in the star center. Draw a paper square with a right angle 18" long, pin to the 18" seam allowance on two adjacent sides of star, and draw the arc. Note that I was working with leftover decorator remnants, so I had to draft a creative "serendipity" design.

I simply backed this table skirt with a muslin sheet sans batting. It hangs beautifully on a 27" diameter table, draping down 25".

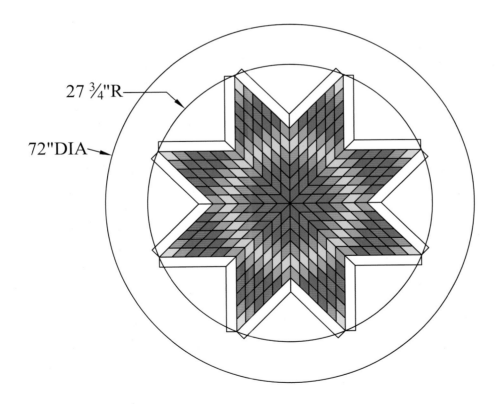

27 ¾"R

72"DIA

Lone Star Wall Hanging (Holiday Style)

60" × 42½"

Cutting:

Choose a selection of five fabrics in holiday colors or a selection of your choice. Cut a rectangle 12" × 36" for each color. Extra four pieced star points for border: 12" × 21". For each of these five fabrics, cut five strips 2¼" wide. Label the fabrics 1 through 5. Stack them in preparation for stitching 1 through 5 (Group A), then 2 through 1 (Group B), then 3 through 2 (Group C), then 4 through 3 (Group D), then 5 through 4 (Group E).

I fussy cut the center eight diamonds for a kaleidoscope effect.

Cut four background fabrics 13" square for corners. Cut one square 19" and divide on the diagonal both ways for four setting triangles. Note: A 1" (½" finished) accent is sewn and flipped on the outside edges of corner squares and also the long side on the four triangles, requiring 4½ yards.

Addendum cuts:

Due to the fact that people take various seam allowances, the set in triangles and squares may vary. To find out the perfect large square (this yields four triangles cut on both diagonals) and the corner square cuts, measure from the actual ¼" inside sewing line to the inside star point.

The formula for the squares and triangles for any Lone Star background is:

1. Measure the finished outside edge of the pieced diamond. I do this more than one side to get a happy medium, as some sides with bias have some stretch.

2. For the corner squares, add ½" or 0.5 and cut four squares.

3. For the large squares that will be cut on each diagonal, yielding four triangles, multiply the finished edge × 2 and multiply that number × .707 (length of right angle) + 1¼" (1.25).

11", cut four squares 11½" Large square cut 17"

11¼", cut four squares 11¾" Large square cut 17¼"

11½", cut four squares 12" Large square cut 17½"

12", cut four squares 12½" Large square cut 18¼"

12¼", cut four squares 12¾" Large square cut 18⅝"

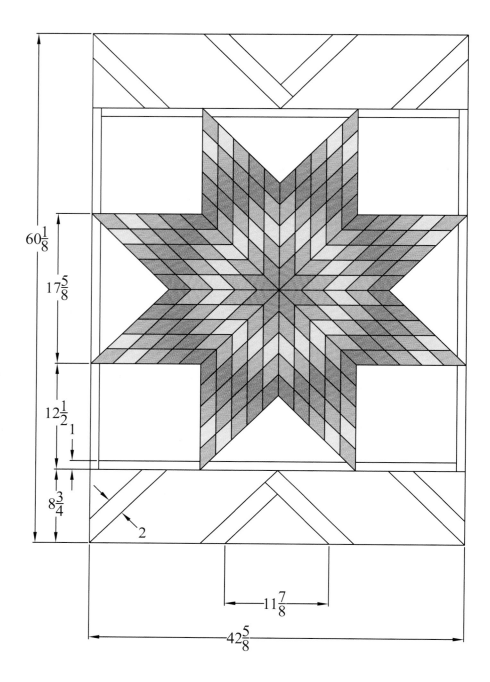

Cut eight diagonal accent bands for border 2½" × 13¼", with a 45-degree angle cut at each long end to make a trapezoid. Note that these angle edges will be on the bias. The middle triangle is cut from a 9¼" square with one diagonal cut. The end triangles are cut from two squares 6⅞", with one diagonal cut in each for the four triangles.

Method:

Sew Groups A through E together, staggering each new strip 2". Start with #1 through #5; sew the next group #2, #3, #4, #5, and #1; sew the next group #3, #4, #5, #1, and #2, etc.

Press all closed seams in alternate direction, using the "innies" and "outies" technique. Note how Group A seams are opposite pressing to Group B. Using the 45-degree angle on a ruler, cut apart each band 2¼" (3½" on the straight edge, not the bias). Hint: With masking tape, mark the 45-degree along with the 2¼" for repeat cuts.

Taking one strip from each group, pin the star together eight times. Pin and peek at each intersection, allowing for seams that are aligned when stitched. "Unpick" the stitches from the raw edge to the sewn seam for a twirling intersection. Press for a flat seam.

Sew in sets of two points each. At the outside right angle, sew only up to the ¼", then stop and backstitch. Sew in halves. Press connecting diamond seams in the same direction on the backside. Pin center so the seams are staggered. Complete center seam and then twirl center intersection by releasing stitches from raw edges to the center seam.

Sew the outside triangles into place four times. Align the 45-degree angles and sew up to the inside ¼", then backstitch to secure. The corner squares can be sewn in by aligning the right angles and sewing up to the inside ¼" seam and back stitching.

Binding Requirements: 6 yards of 2¼" wide cut fabric.

60-Degree Diamond: Diamond Dazzle Quilt

77¼" × 100½"

The 60-degree diamond, like the Lone Star 45-degree diamond, is another classic in our quilt repertoire. Here, a coveted border print from my stash becomes the inspiration for the center star, accents, and border. The "baby block" complexes expand outward in a medley of scrap fabrics composed of dark, medium, and light. Ease in piecing is relieved by splitting the diamond to create rows, thus eliminating the major "Y" intersections.

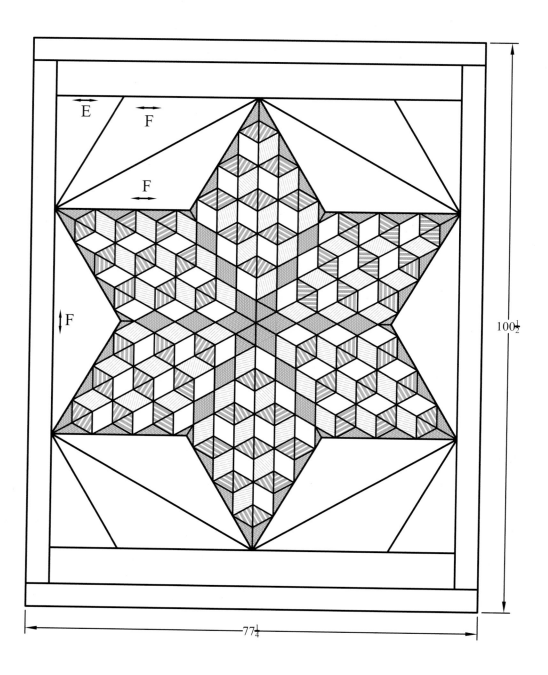

Fabric Requirements:

1 yard of medium and 1 yard of light fabric for A and B diamonds

1 yard of dark fabric for the D diamonds

1/2 yard for accent C diamonds and side triangles

1 yard each of two contrasting fabrics for setting triangles (F and E)

2 yards of border print fabric or focus fabric

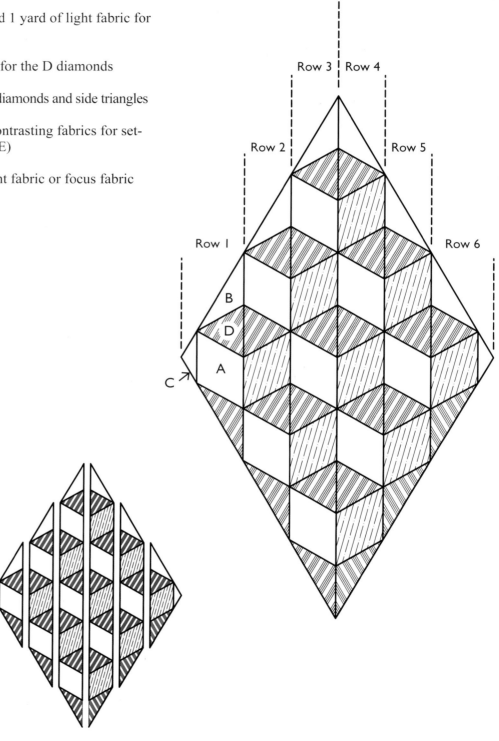

Cutting:

Template free, strip cutting, based on 42" selvage to selvage.

Cut 16 accent A diamonds by cutting three rows of strips across fabric 4" wide. Each row yields eight A diamonds that include seam allowances. Use the 60-degree angle on a ruler every 4". Hint: Marking the ruler with temporary masking tape helps in each of the cutting turns. Cut four accent D triangles.

Cut 54 light and medium A diamonds by cutting nine strips across fabric 4" wide. Each row yields eight A diamonds; that includes seam allowances. For a scrap look, select various shades of light and various shades of medium. Use the 60-degree angle on ruler every 4".

Cut 108 dark D triangles by cutting eight rows across 4¼" wide. Each row yields 15 D triangles that include seam allowances. For a scrap look, select various shades of dark strips. Use the 60-degree angle on ruler to turn each time, creating the equilateral D triangle.

Cut 36 side setting B triangles by cutting across five strips 2⅝" wide. Each row yields eight triangles. Use the 30-degree angle on the ruler, turning each time for the B triangles.

Cut 12 side setting C triangles by cutting across 1 strip 1¾" wide. Use the 30-degree angles of the ruler, turning each time for the C triangles: one strip yields 12 required triangles.

Diamond Dazzle E & F Measurements

	Quilt, 4" Diamond	Wall Hanging, 3" Diamond
A	23⅛"	12⅛"
B	11½"	6"
C	40"	21"
D	20"	10½"

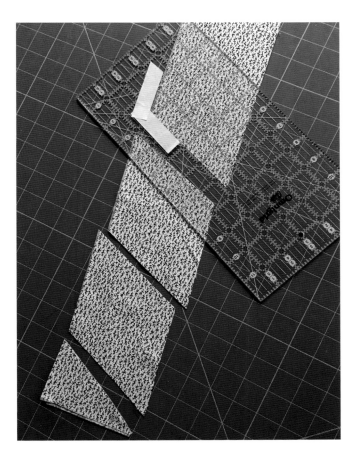

A diamond.

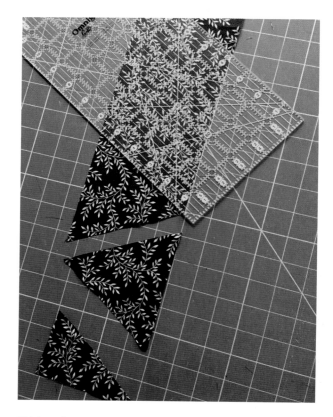

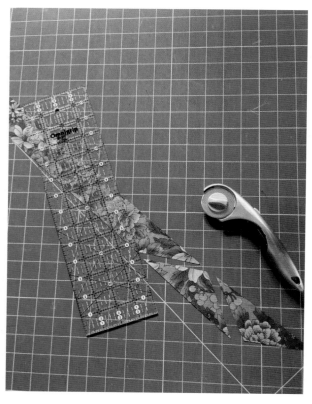

D triangle.

C triangle.

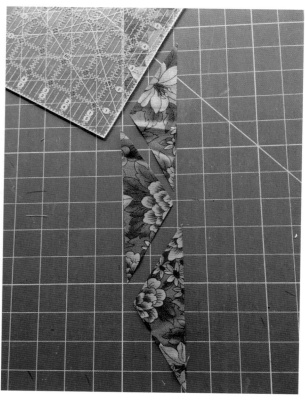

Set up for 30 angle cuts 2⅝" width.

B triangle.

Referring to the E and F templates measurement diagram, make the E and F background triangles from Grid Grip or freezer paper. Once cut out, press onto fabric aligning grain lines on fabric. Note that F side triangles have straight of grain on the long side of triangle. Add seam allowances on all sides of templates when cutting.

The F template can be joined for one large diamond rather than two.

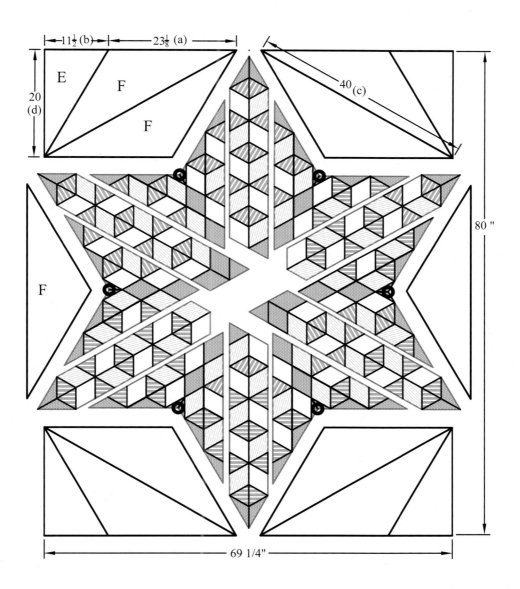

Method:

For star assembly, stitch six double rows of diamonds and triangles. Stack the D triangle with alternating A light and medium diamonds, following the row schematic. Pin the D triangle so that once sewn and flipped 64 times, the outside is on the straight of the grain. Sew these rows together, alternating the seams, up versus down, on each row. Note where these rows position in the overall schematic.

Stitch together the six point connector segments, following the explosion diagram.

Start by sewing together the center star rows. Press all the center star seams in the same direction in order to twirl the seam allowances for a soft center. Then sew together the five units on each side of the center section. Secure them for a final stitch. Stop at the ¼" seam allowance on all of the obtuse C triangles indicated on the schematic with a small dark circle.

BINDING REQUIREMENTS:
10 yards of 2¼" wide cut fabric.

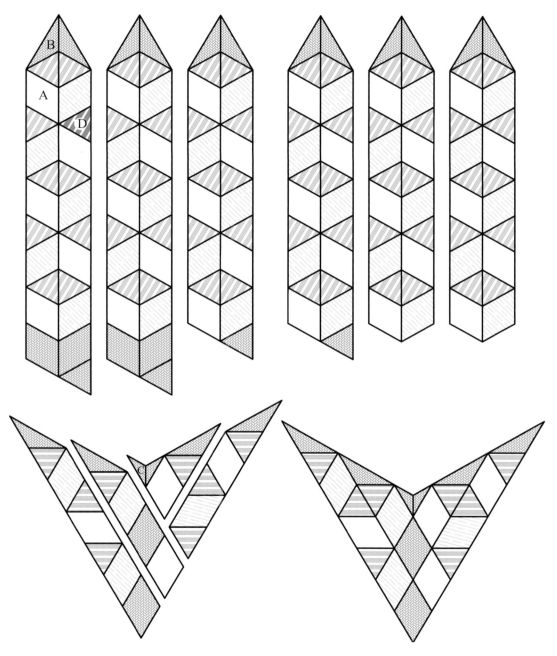

4" diamonds.

Diamond Dazzle Wall Hanging

36¼" × 42" (3" diamond)

Cutting:

Cut 10 accent A diamonds (four could be dark) by cutting one strip 3⅛" wide. Using the 60-degree angle on the ruler, cut out 10 diamonds every 3⅛" apart. Cut four accent D triangles.

Cut 24 light and medium A diamonds by cutting three strips 3⅛" wide. Using the 60-degree angle on the ruler, cut out 24 A diamonds for each.

Cut 48 dark D triangles by cutting strips 3½" wide. Using the 60-degree angle on the ruler, turning each time, cut out 18 triangles for each row.

Cut four D triangles from the accent fabric (four could be dark).

Cut 24 side setting B triangles by cutting two strips plus another half a strip 2" wide. Using the 30-degree angle on the ruler, turning each time, cut 10 triangles for each strip.

Cut 12 side setting C triangles by cutting one strip 1½" wide. Using the 30-degree angle of the ruler, cut out 12 triangles from the strip.

Cut four 4 E triangles and 10 F triangles, referring to the dimensions given on the E and F template measurement chart. Mark grain lines and note that the side triangles have the grain line on the long side of the triangles. Note that two F templates can form one single diamond; in which case, cut 4.

BINDING REQUIREMENTS:
4½ yards of 2¼" wide cut fabric.

Quick cutting instructions are given for A, B, C, and D pieces. If using the templates A, B, C, and D, add ¼" seam allowance on all sides.

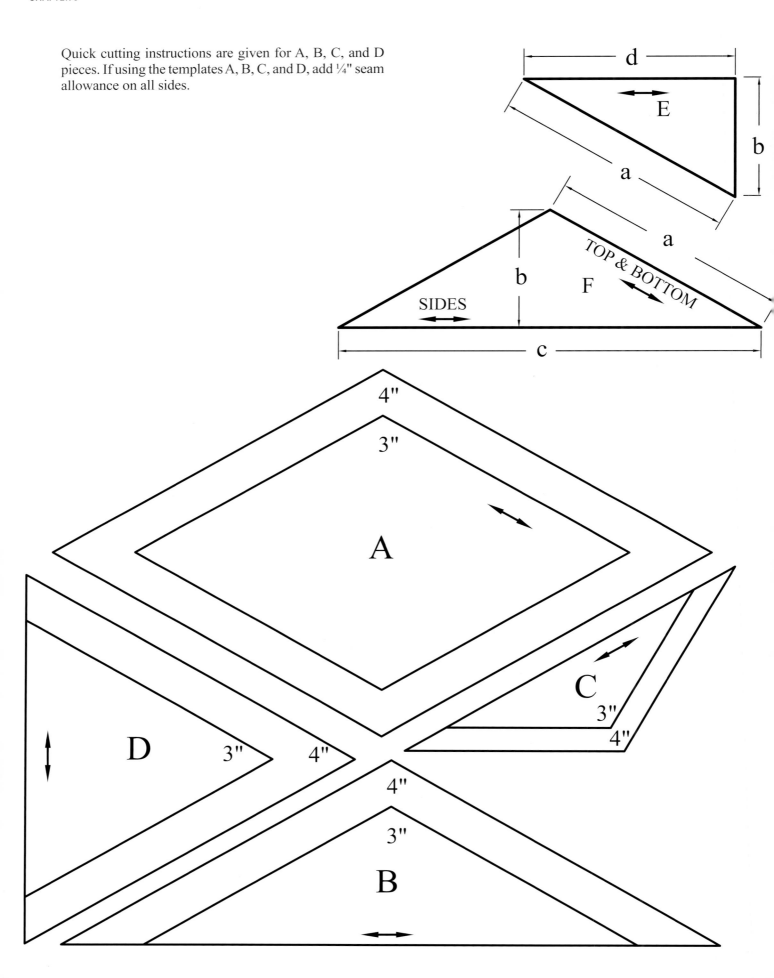

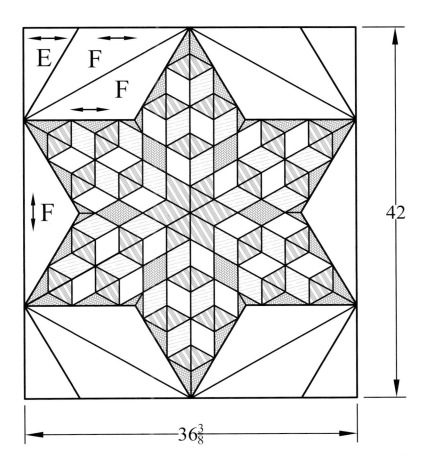

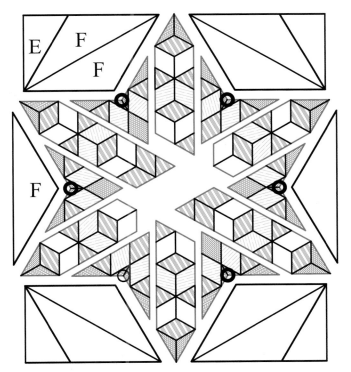

Wall Hanging, 36¼" × 42" (3" diamonds).

Sunflowers à la Marie Webster Quilt

87½" × 98½"

"Quilts are not only for remembering, but reliving their making." The Sunflower quilt by Marie Webster was first published in the January 1912 issue of *Ladies' Home Journal*. It is worthy of repeating, but with a different slant: machine pieced with machine appliqué flowers. In this newer rendition, tall sunflowers with their stems are rooted in an angled border and radiate toward a center panel.

This quilt became a week's project at our Montreat retreat, with many interesting variations. It always makes a teacher proud when the students add their own flair. A notable smaller rendition uses the four corners for a wall hanging.

Some quilts simply age well on a quilt studio wall and become "works in progress."

Pat Ditella's sunflower quilt in progress.

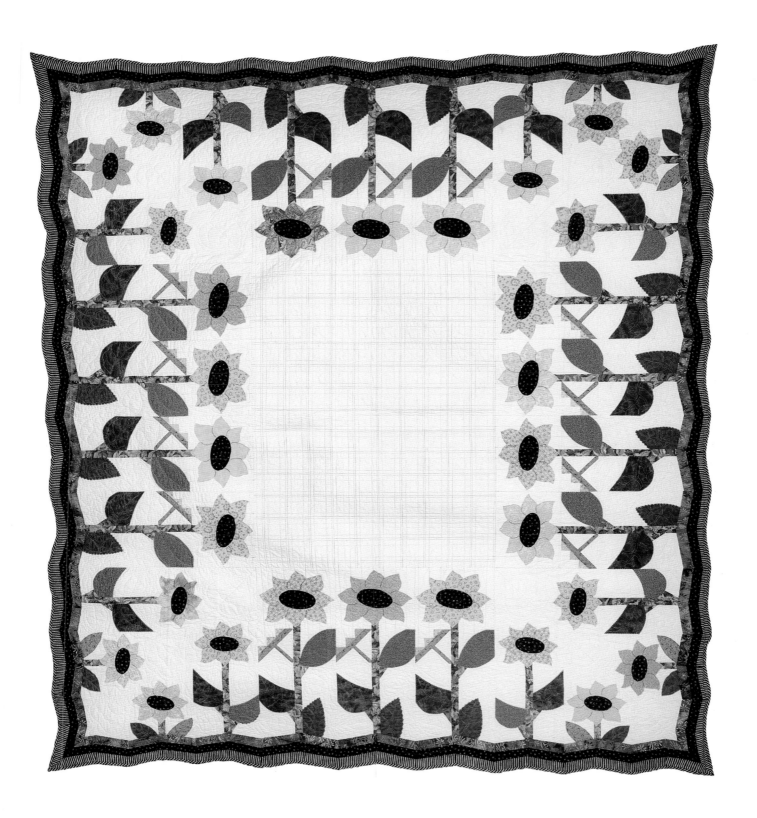

Materials:

Background fabric plus center rectangle: 8 yards

Stems: ½ yard

Green leaves, various shades: 2 yards

Oval center for sunflowers: ½ yard

Sunflowers: 1¾ yards of various yellows

Backing: (I quilted this in sections on my Bernina, with a different shade of yellow fabric for each of the nine sections.)
9 1-yard pieces of yellow-shaded fabric

Border: ¾ yard of two different colors

Method:

I machine quilted this quilt in nine sections, which made it practical to break down the center panel, sunflower panels, and the corners. The center panel was machine quilted in continuous directional plaid lines with variegated thread from Charlotte Warr Andersen's book *One Line at a Time* (C&T Publishing). The original quilt had clamshell and spiderweb quilting lines.

Cut this panel along with batting and backing, 44" × 33½". Baste and machine quilt in your favorite pattern. Trim this panel to 42½" × 32", which includes the seam allowance.

Cut out necessary templates for the 14-sunflower, leaf-and-stem rectangular panel.

The small bud square, 5¼" (finished 4¾") uses five templates. Cut and stich all 14 of these. There is a left-side leaf section, marked L, and a right-side leaf section, marked R, with stem A in between. Sew together according to the number sequence, starting with #1, noting some challenging curves to stitch. Remember, there is always hand piecing for these seams! Stitch each of the L and R panels to the center A stem, stopping ¼" from the top, backstitch in place. This leaves a loose stem to secure after the rectangle is attached.

Cut out 14 sunflower background rectangles, 9½" × 11½", to be trimmed to 9" × 11" once the appliqué is complete. This allows for any takeup from the appliqué. Either hand or machine sew the sunflower onto the background. My method was machine satin stitch for the flower and the center oval.

Trace B sunflower onto freezer paper. Press it onto an array of yellow fabric selections, cutting out about a ¼" seam allowance. Position the template on the rectangle, noting the hash lines to match grain lines, and straight stitch the flower onto the light foundation, using the paper edge as a guide place to follow. Mark the area where the stem from the leaf panel will slip under the flower, and leave that open. With lip appliqué scissors, trim off the excess seam allowance. With a stabilizer or paper underneath, against the feed dogs, zigzag on top of the straight line of stitching.

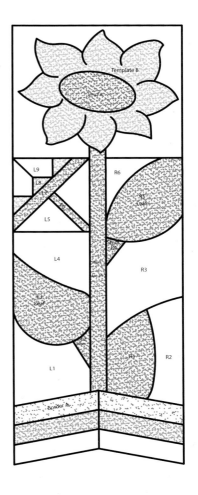

See the Patterns & Templates section for more.

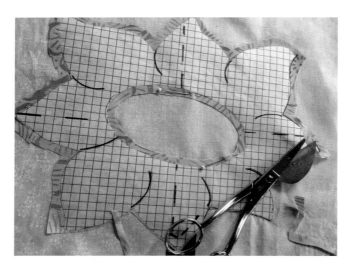

Sunflower template pressed in place to stitch around edge and cut away ¼" extension.

Finished edges of flower with zigzag stitches covering initial straight stitching.

Complete the sunflower with an appliqué dark center, template A, securing in the same manner as above. For extra flair I hand sewed yellow shiny beads in this area. Trim the rectangles to 9" × 11" and stitch to all 14 leaf panels. Hand appliqué the sides of the stem, then trim and insert under the flower. Complete the straight stitching and satin stitch here.

Cut out and stitch the corners. The sunflowers use template D and center oval template C. Follow the directions (Template F) for cutting out background fabric. Using a variety of scrap green fabric separates the leaves, as four times they do touch each other once sewn together.

Add the triple border A, B, and C to the base of all sunflower panels.

With the two panels of four, the two panels of three, and the corners, the machine quilting can begin. I selected various shades of yellow for each backing. Choose your favorite way of basting and quilting. Leave any inside connecting edges at least ½" free of quilting. When basting the sunflower panels I removed any batting ¼" from any connecting edges. I had three horizontal rows with the side four-panel sunflowers attached first after quilting.

BINDING REQUIREMENTS:
10½ yards of 2¼" wide cut fabric.

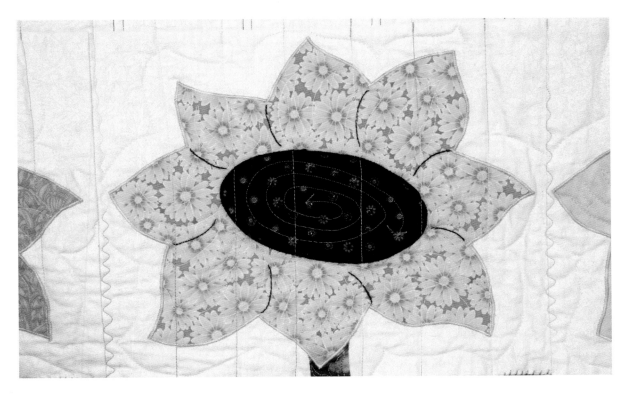

Completed flower.

Not Everyone Likes Sunflowers, by Lorraine Tritthardt.
Sometimes a full quilt is just intimidating, so here is
another option—just the corners, and in pink.

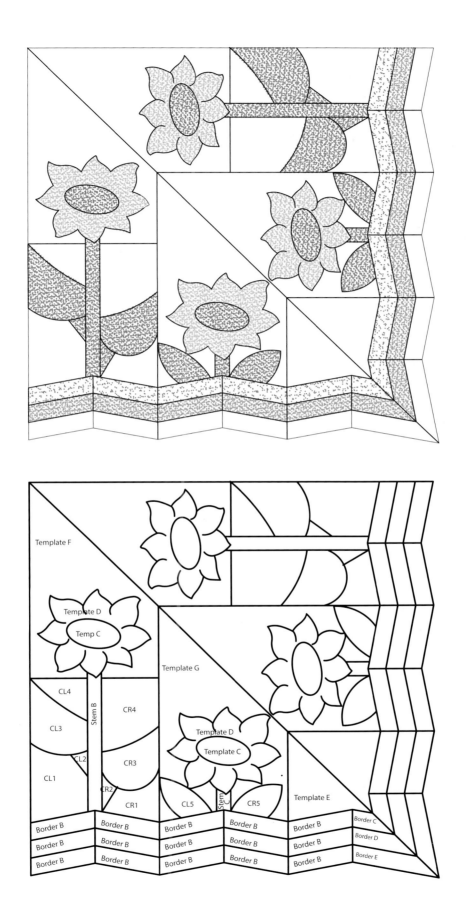

Live simply,

Love generously,

Care deeply,

Speak kindly,

And leave the rest to God.

—Ronald Reagan

4 The Teacher

It has been my good fortune and privilege to be a part of the quilt-making community through teaching. I believe that the need to create is inborn with women and men as the creators of life itself. The wonder of fabric and design emerging in a quilt top is very soul satisfying and lends a sense of productivity to our home scene. There are so many lessons to be learned, but you have to live them first and benefit from the mistakes.

Quilters share, they boast, they brag, they often bring fabrics for a class that match what they are wearing, they compete in a nice way, and they want to finish. It is something about self-worth and being with like-minded people that can form the sole incentive.

At a 1979 North Carolina Quilt Symposium, a person commented on an unusual knot she learned while sitting in a lecture, a knot shown by a lady with an English accent. "Show me," I said, and that is when I learned the quilter's foolproof knot that I have taught for years on TV and in the classroom. Confirming the importance of that knot came in a letter from the wife of a surgeon. "It really surprised me to see his eyes open wide and sparkle as he realized the possibilities which you showed of drawing the knot down the thread. Apparently he held a demonstration the very next day in the lab! He implants pacemakers, so there are doubtless many more bodies than those of quilters who are indebted to you," wrote Karen. The fan mail and correspondence I have received over the years is a testimony to people's pride and love of quilt making. Nowadays, of course, these are emails.

I have learned that the most creative quilt you will make is when you mess up the supply list, or (even worse) when, heaven forbid, the teacher gets the list wrong. I recall a class in West Virginia where a student appeared with floral print for the sky and just stitched away until she had a quite remarkable mountain scene. Who said flowers can't float in the sky?

So often, students will underestimate their own powers. With a little instruction, encouragement, and gentle coaxing, women and men find renewed confidence in their own abilities. Soon they are exclaiming, "Look,

I did it myself." (Unlike the student who did not return to class, commenting, "Oh, I didn't know it was so much work.") Yes, I am the first to admit that it takes energy, time, and money to make a quilt, but the important part is that lessons are learned every step along the way.

One of the more exciting teaching efforts was done with the Alleghany Quilters Guild from Sparta, North Carolina, who contacted me about a teapot quilt. Now, that was not on my design bucket list, but there was a need, so before I knew it we were meeting in Hickory, North Carolina. It gave me a chance to brag on the benefits of gridded freezer paper and help them contribute to their art efforts in the community (www.hickoryart.org). I offer one of the teapot blocks to you here, to challenge you to design more from the quilt.

WHAT I LEARNED:

Teaching is a two-way street with enthusiasm and confidence as the keys.

The Teapot Quilt

Teapot Block: 10" block

Add ¼" seam allowance to all sides of each template. Piecing is done in four sections, A through D. In each instance, start with the smallest number: A1 to A2, etc., then B1 to B2, etc.

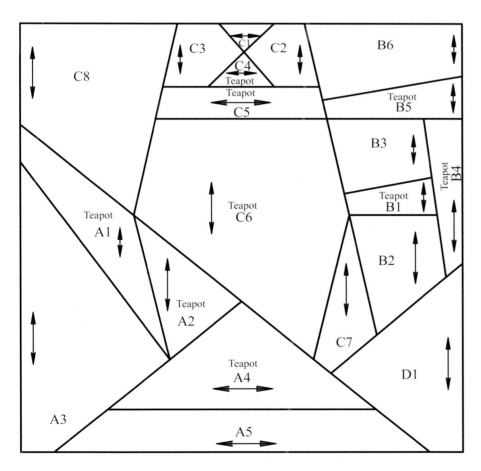

The schematic for the 10" block. It offers a fancier handle. You can make a simpler version if you prefer, as shown in the photo. Notice the mirror image effect that is created by reversing the teapot.

See the Patterns & Templates section for more.

Imitation might be the sincerest form of flattery,

but making a mistake is the truest form of creativity.

—GB

The Guild Member & Quilt Groupies

There is a direct relation between the amount of time devoted to your guild and your final enjoyment. When you belong to three local guilds, it's all about time. I am proud to be a founding president of the Western North Carolina Quilt Guild and founding member of two other guilds, the Landrum Guild and the Asheville Quilt Guild, but time does not permit me to attend all meetings. I have such a history with each of these guilds and people.

The Landrum Guild was and still is important, as my parents retired to the area. I featured the guild on one of the television shows taped at the library where the group met. Soon people would appear at our

hardware store and claim, "I knew I was in quilt country when I saw the Landrum sign on the highway." Once when I couldn't conduct the class, I asked my mother to sub for me. She ran out of things to say in 20 minutes of that three-hour class!

Each of our area quilt guilds has become known for giving back to the community. The list is long and varied, including kits provided for charity that include patterns, fabric, and batting; the quilts are completed for causes like Project Linus, local hospitals, North Carolina Veterans Home, Meals on Wheels, Habitat for Humanity, preemie hats for the NICU, and care partners in hospice.

Our Little Circle of the World quilt by Western North Carolina Quilt Guild. It is on display at our local courthouse in Hendersonville, North Carolina. Over the years I've been able to donate three opportunity quilts to the WNCQ Guild. (This quilt was made by members from the leftover Postage Stamp quilt 1½" squares. You might recall the cover quilt on the book *Bright Ideas*.)

God Save the Queen wall hanging, 28" × 28". Promoting
the guild and giving back to the community are
important features of the WNCQ guild. They celebrate
National Quilt Day with an exhibit that presents an
annual challenge. One year it was to use the first letter of
your name; hence the "G," plus I am an anglophile with
a huge collection of buttons.

What proves beneficial are the small groups of quilters that are part of the larger picture, often referred to as "groupies." So let me brag about three groupies, beginning with the Cover Lovers.

In North Carolina, quilts have long been referred to as kivers, but how could a new quilt group be called kiver livers when Cover Lovers had a much better ring to it? After all, we love our covers just as well.

This nucleus of ardent new quilters evolved from a community college class conducted in my home studio. They learned how to adapt patchwork to garments but were not willing to end the studies, so 30 years later, twice a month we still get together in members' homes. Together we have experienced every phase of life, truly a support group woven between threads.

Now we even explore knitting patterns and exchange new fiber ideas. In 1985, when I experienced my acoustic neuroma brain surgery (www.anausa.org), these were the ladies who sang Christmas carols outside our door on a very cold winter's evening. I will never forget their compassion. I have found such support and renewal with these people and feel so fortunate to have them in our lives.

Every group has its own character, derived from the individual members. My PTA, Professional Textile Artists (alias Patchwork, Talking, and Appliqué) group has a gentle, competitive air to each get-together. Why? It is made up almost entirely of teachers and members of the Southern Highland Craft Guild. I do believe the caliber of our individual efforts is elevated just having that friendly "one-up-womanship" atmosphere. We believe in challenges and set themes that evolve into collections of fiber art for exhibition and sales.

One year the invitation set forth was for the theme of stamps with a unified scalloped border. Mine was Patchwork Forever with my own QR reader, a real challenge to piece! Showing off is part of our thing. Yes, you can find comfort in your own capabilities, but expanding is not out of the realm with smart ladies. Nothing like healthy competition to spur on quilters enhancing their own workmanship. The results of quilt challenges highlight pushing the creative power of patchwork.

Imagine the same quilt class meeting annually for over 30 years; that is my Freedom Escape class. When I bragged on this annual event to a group in Houston, a gentleman spoke up: "And they haven't learned yet?" The fact that the students return year after year is a credit to the personal bond between class members, a connection to quilt making, and the allure of a new project each year.

Twice, we brought the NC Public Television crew over to film this class in action for a *Lap Quilting* show (shows 503 and 908). Many of the quilt patterns in *Scrap Happy* saw first life with this accepting group.

WHAT I LEARNED:

Quilt clubs and guilds enhance the community through quilt donations. They thrive on social interaction of like minds and hands discovering ways to learn and share.

Patchwork Forever wall hanging (PTA Challenge), 32" × 42".

Roots wall hanging. 43½" × 57". Linda Cantrell (a PTA
member) and I created this appliqué wall hanging
denoting our PTA group with memorabilia that pertains to
each member. This was the biannual exhibit named
Fellowship, at the Folk Art Center in Asheville.
www.craftguild.org.

Diligence is the mother of good luck.

—Benjamin Franklin

The Circuit Rider

I admire the circuit riders, the teachers who work their lives between family and venturing away from home to share their knowledge. That teachers like this exist speaks well of our quilt community and the dedication and spirit of our craft. When I rode the circuit, every trip was a teaching and learning journey. My sewing machine was always close by, so in my free time I got to stitch away. Some of my best quilts were pieced and even finished on the road. My best advice: keep a diary.

Most of my trips were solo but upon occasion my husband, Pete, came along. On a memorable trip to Australia we took a side trip to watch some amazing native dancers. On the train ride back I was stitching a cathedral quilt block for a chatelaine gift, and before I knew it I was teaching a small group of Chinese ladies right there on the train. Never be afraid to share a sewing skill.

Then we were off to New Zealand and another story. How did we get there? A hometown friend of ours fished in TeAnu every year, and one time relaxing on the porch he spied the owner reading a book. You guessed it, my book. So that became our connection and led to an invitation for me to share my quilt suitcase with her club in exchange for a few days touring the area.

So while Pete toured the sheep lands, I unpacked my big quilt bag for the interested ladies. Then with lunch time approaching we proceeded to fine dining with a promise of a surprise. After lunch we piled into cars and drove to the secret location. At our destination, which was out in a wooded area, near some railroad tracks, they handed me an envelope full of money. "OK, Georgia, now you can bungy jump off the Kawarau Bridge!" Well, I did survey this generous opportunity and witnessed some breathtaking jumps, but ultimately returned the envelope, explaining how much fabric that would buy. Thanks, but no thanks.

Other times you have to get creative to finish a project while on a holiday. I once received a last-minute invitation to a river cruise on the Mississippi but was under a deadline, so I had to bring the project and sewing machine along. Well, it was a fine time but I discovered that once evening comes, when I intended to stitch, the power onboard decreased. I had to switch to daytime sewing in between bridge games and tours. The rooms were too small for a machine setup, so I found a corner in the lounge but was soon fielding constant questions. What are you making? Are you a quilter? Why are you using those colors? Finally,

Centennial Celebration, 2012. 41" × 37".

Detail of horse panel.

I solved the dilemma by just saying, "I am the ship's seamstress." And got my blocks completed. (For my longtime fans, you can find this quilt in your Bonesteel book archives; it was The String Along Lily in *More Lap Quilting*, page 23.) So I learned, never leave your quilting at home.

One of my favorite stories has no moral but is fun to share nevertheless. Once upon a time I taught for Walmart at Lake of the Ozarks.

I also judged quilt blocks from across the country and then instructed sales people in an enormous underground garage. I ended up sitting next to Mr. Walton at dinner. Someone turned to me and said that Mrs. Walton really wanted to play tennis in the morning, and did I play? Well, being a solid B player, I thought it would be fun to take her on. Naturally, since she had to be quite a bit older than myself I contemplated that it would only be proper to give her the edge out on the courts. Well, did she fool me! I kept missing her returns and spent most of the time apologizing. Let it be known that she cleaned my clock and will go down in my little history book as a really good tennis player.

Another time I had two hours in the Denver airport without any thread, but I was desperate to finish a quilt. No problem; I simply unwove an edge of the extended backing and pulled the fabric apart to be used as thread. At least I had a needle and scissors.

Montana has been a special place for our family. How wonderful to have a western home at a ranch, even for just a week every year. Teaching there has its own challenges. These classes shared with coteacher Charlotte Warr Andersen are limited to two days and divided among hiking, fishing, horseback riding, and touring quilt shops. Learning how to size up the differences of each situation has made me a more adaptable teacher and quilter. Now I have a collection of quilts, wall hangings, and novelty fiber art with a western influence. What will next year bring? Will it be an animal, bird, landscape, or maybe horseshoes? Centennial Celebration pays respect for the 100 years of the Nine Quarter Circle Ranch's existence as we taught, jointly, a special wall hanging. Two other favorites that you can make are Moon Over Mt. Eagle and Add a Bunny.

I am not alone in being the traveling quilter. Just examine the quilter who's heading off to a local class or jetting off across the country. They are well packed and equipped with devices, notions, fabric, and machines. More power to all circuit riders, be they teacher or student.

WHAT I LEARNED:
Expand your quilt panorama on the road, using trips as a springboard for new stimulus. Whether it was teaching or filming, it was all about learning, and do not forget your camera.

Nine Quarter Circle Trophy. 24" × 34".

Comedy/Tragedy Quilt

31" × 31"

When quilts leave the bed they take on new opportunities to warm not only the walls, but the hearts as well. What better way to display fiber art and declare your passion?

The wave of blocks on buildings and barns is sweeping the country. This graphic art responds to history, culture, and family instincts. The Mask; Comedy and Tragedy block (4' × 4') is the first installation in Henderson County, North Carolina, with more to come in our Quilt Trails of Western North Carolina.

My concept of comedy and tragedy was further fine-tuned by designer Martin Webster. His wife, Barbara Webster, has been instrumental in launching this Burnsville, North Carolina, group (www.quilttrailswnc.org). Since this initial concept from Donna Sue Groves in Ohio, many states have followed in these footsteps to enhance and beautify neighborhoods and country roads. Making the design in a 31" smaller fabric size allows having your own Mask as a wall hanging.

Comedy (C1–C8 templates) and Tragedy (T1–T8 templates) Wall Hanging is based on four 14" blocks. (Add ¼" seam allowance around all templates.)

Fabric Requirements:

For four 14" blocks: ½ yard of light and ½ yard of dark fabric.

Corner Triangles: (T8) Cut two dark and two light squares 7¼"; cut on the diagonal.

Put wrong or right sides of fabric together, cutting out two fabrics with one template.

Select fabric that is reversible such as solid colored or batik.

Grid Grip works great here by copying the templates onto the paper. Also draw the rectangle T3.

Method:

1. Cut out this rectangle (all the C templates pressed onto fabric) and layer onto a second layered set in order to cut out two blocks at one time. Cut out templates, adding the ¼" seam allowance on all sides. Arrange blocks in preparation for stitching with corner triangles. Stitch blocks together according to #1, #2, etc.

2. Complete each of the C 14" (14½" with seam allowances) blocks by adding the contrasting C8 triangles.

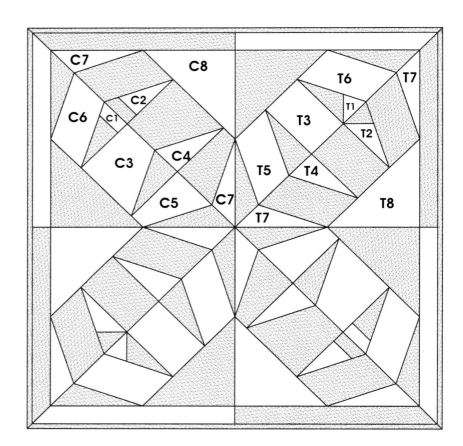

See the Patterns & Templates section for more.

3. Insert picture of laid-out cut templates before stitching.

4. Repeat the above using the T templates until all four blocks are complete, ending with the T8 contrasting triangles.

5. Sew halves together and then complete as a four patch.

6. Add accent ledges on all four sides of blocks. Cut four strips 1" × 28½" long. Turn under ends ¼" and press in half. Baste or pin with the fold leaning inward, allowing ¼" at each end for mitering. Cut four dark and four light strips 2½" × 17", sewing one light and one dark together four times end to end. Stagger the contrasting borders; attach and miter the ends. My wall hanging was hand quilted using various widths of masking tape as guides.

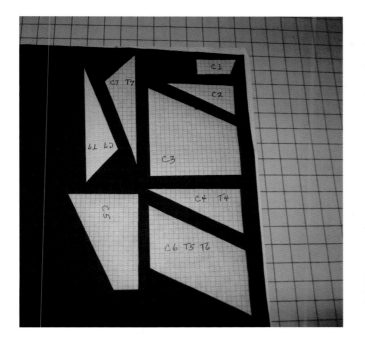

The Barn Collection Quilts

30" × 38"

These four wall hangings are a series of barn quilts made to inspire at one of my Freedom Escape weeklong retreats. Only a few students took the bait and copied the teacher, since so many had barn memories of their own. We were able to create an exhibit of about 35 quilts in Burnsville at a Chevy car dealership. Great show with even a cardboard mannequin of James Dean leaning over the balcony. What about yourself? Do you have a fond barn memory? Maybe these wall hangings will jump-start your pencil and rotary cutter.

Star Barn

30" × 38"

Star Barn wall hanging is based on 6" quarter-square triangles. It is a 25 patch with five 6" squares across and five 6" squares down.

Fabric Requirements and Cutting:

1. Sky: 10 quarter-square triangles made from several sky scrap fabrics. Cut five sets of 7½" squares. Draw a diagonal line on the back side of each set; stitch a ¼" seam on either side of the line; cut apart on the pencil line; press closed seams in one direction (keep four pieced triangles apart as two go on either side of the roof and the other unstitches for a roof triangle); place right sides together, staggering seam allowances; draw another diagonal line on the back side; stitch on either side and cut apart to reveal nine squares. Trim all five half-square triangles to 6½" squares. Also trim four pieced triangles.

2. Windmill: Cut four 6" squares and fold into a prairie point (fold on the diagonal once and then again); pin in place with raw edges aligned to be sewn in row assembly.

3. Rooster: Using rooster pattern, cut out and appliqué or fuse in place along with the stem.

4. Star Barn: Make four quarter-square triangles from a yellow/brown combination. Cut two yellow and two brown squares 7½". Follow directions from step 1, making four blocks. Trim all to 6½" squares.

5. Barn: Cut two brown and two other print 7½". Make four quarter-square triangles. Note that one square is left as a pieced triangle for the roof area, to be sewn to the sky pieced triangles. Trim to 6½" squares.

6. Center Square: Cut rectangle 3½" × 6½"; cut square 3⅞" and cut apart on the diagonal; cut a right angle triangle with a base on the straight of grain 7¼".

7. Grass: Cut four grass/ground fabric sets 7½". Make eight quarter-square triangles. Only seven are needed, so save the extra for the label on back. Trim to 6½" squares.

8. With all segments cut and stitched, sew the Star Barn together in rows, starting with row #1. Insert prairie points in row #1 and #2. Appliqué seven dark strips cut 1" wide as supports for the windmill. Some areas will need to be unstitched, allowing the supports to be slipped inside and restitched.

9. Appliqué road marker and pole in place. I embroidered the 19 with a chain stitch, using six strands of thread.

Road Border Accents for Top and Bottom of all four Barn wall hangings:

Cut four white strips: 30½" × ¾"

Cut four dark strips: 2" × 30½"

Cut two yellow strips: 1" × 30½"

Finishing Method:

Backing fabric cut 30½" × 38½": Put right sides together and stitch top and bottom with a ¼" seam. Invert and bind the sides. Note how I matched the binding (cut 2¼" wide, pressed and folded) to the background areas for the Star Barn. All three other barns have their own continuous binding.

Barns from Schematics

The following barns are all drawn with measurements given on a schematic.

Allow yourself any margin of error as long as you get the essence of the barn. The line drawn on freezer paper or Grid Grip will indicate the exact sewing line once cut out and pressed onto the chosen fabric. Once pressed onto fabric; add seam allowances for piecing.

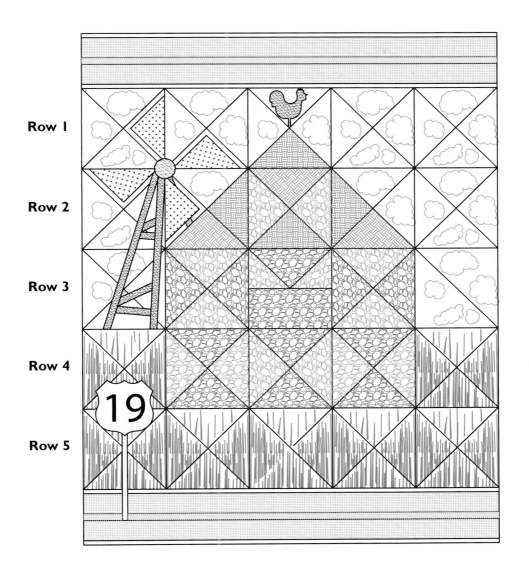

Row 1

Row 2

Row 3

Row 4

Row 5

See the Patterns &
Templates section
for more.

View from Below

30" × 38"

Fabric Requirements and Cutting:

1. Following the schematic, draw the slanted barn on a 30" square of Grid Grip or freezer paper. It is possible to overlap the paper and press together. Identify the A through H templates and place the windows with pencil and then indelible fine-line pen. The B area is an 11½" top opening for a slanted (60-degree angle) block of your choice. The Twinkle Toes block is given here.

2. Cut out templates and press on to chosen fabrics. Red fabric is cut 1½" wide with a 60-degree angle and pieced together for the actual size plus seam allowances. Stitch A, B (chosen block), and C together. Cut out windows and machine appliqué to D template with additional red strip piecing.

3. Add white accents of trim to the angled roof lines that are attached to the blue sky by stitching in the ditch.

4. Complete the barn with road border accents.

Quilting was stitched in the ditch, echoing the angled piecing and the roof lines.

Directional arrows on a post are accents for your own adaptation.

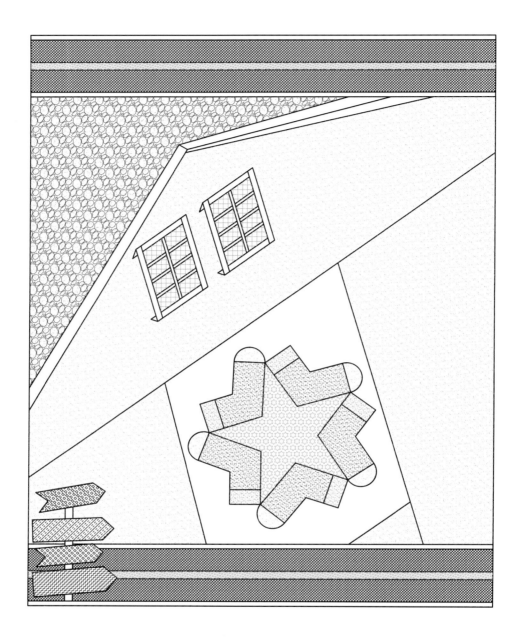

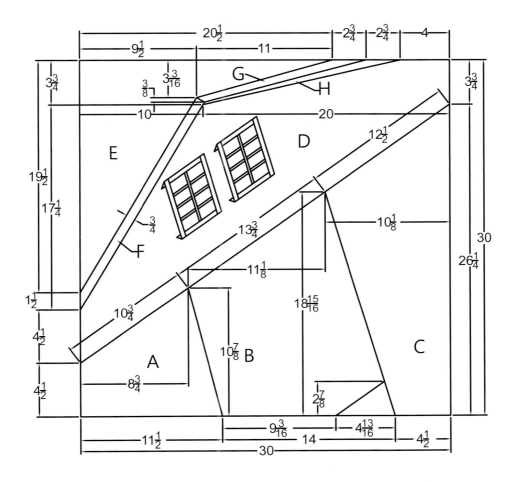

See the Patterns &
Templates section
for more.

Barn with Tractor
30" × 38"

Fabric Requirements and Cutting:

1. Following the schematic, draw the rectangular barn and slanted roof on a Grid Grip or freezer paper cut 24" × 20⅛". Draw the center barn door, hayloft window, and small peak area. Note that the roof is divided in half, making it easier to piece. Choose a half-yard of red for the barn.

2. Cut templates apart, press onto selected fabric, add ¼" seam allowance on all sides, and stitch together. Hayloft window is machine appliquéd in place.

3. Cut out two side panels for sky background 3½" × 23½" and sew to either barn side.

4. Tractor: Transfer A through G templates onto freezer paper, cut out each template, and press onto fabric choices, adding the ¼" seam allowance on all sides. (I was able to select some sister prints of polka dot fabric for the tractor, barn door, windows, and triangular lower border.) Piece the front and back tractor wheels and then attach to the C body. Keep templates in place on fabric outside as a guide to stitch tractor to barn. Cut out 1" strips to be machine stitched as steering, back seat, and vertical pipe on tractor, using a ¼" straight stitch. Trim off the excess and zigzag in place. Stitch the tractor at the base of the barn and trim excess seam allowances, finishing with a satin stitch on top of the raw edges.

5. The six windows are cut 1½" square; the rectangle is 1½" × 3".

6. Top triangle border using the G template: cut six blue G; cut five light blue and two half G (add seam allowance) for the end templates. Piece this row and sew on the top border.

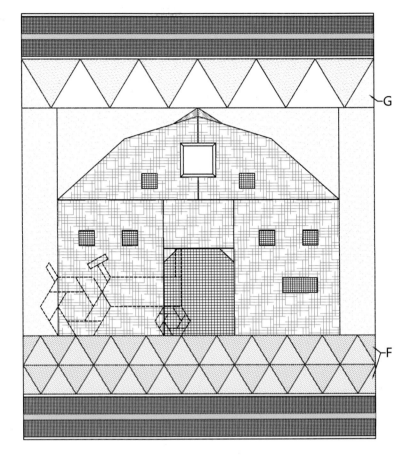

7. Bottom triangle double border using F triangle; cut 19 gold F triangles; cut 19 F green triangles; cut two gold and two green half F triangles (add seam allowance) for each end of the double rows. Piece the triangles, alternating colors.

8. Complete the barn with road border accents.

A small, 3" pieced and bordered star block accents the hayloft area. Machine quilting echoes the print fabric of the barn and sky background.

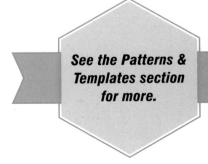

See the Patterns & Templates section for more.

Gray Barn with Red Roof

The inspiration for this barn was seeing this aged barn set in a holler off a country road with a bright graphic quilt block. My picture became the photo transfer to fabric appliquéd twice on the barn façade.

Fabric Requirements and Cutting:

1. Following the schematic, draw the barn measurements on a 30" square of prepared Grid Grip or freezer paper. These become the templates for pressing and cutting out each fabric piece, with the ¼" seam allowance on all sides. Gather your weathered-looking gray fabric to make about 20 strips cut 1" to 1½" × 30". Piece these together for a size larger than the D barn template. Then press this on the right side, adding the ¼" seam allowance. Pressing on the backside will cause the seams to ravel once the paper is peeled off the backing. Cut out the red roof, B and C landscapes, and the A driveway. Select an array of green-tone trees and background. Press 1 through 17 templates on this wavy band of trees, cut out with the ¼" seam allowance. Cut out the three background areas.

2. Stitch barn, roof, and B and C landscapes together. Machine appliqué the driveway in place. Sew the tree band together, adding the background below and above. Secure the barn and roof by cutting out bias strips 1" × 30" in gray and 1" × 20" in red. Fold these in half with the right side out, align raw edges, sew, and flip outward. Use the ditch created to sew in the ditch and apply the barn and roof to the background. The fabric pictures were pieced into the rows.

3. Since this barn was located on road 200 I created an oval road sign and hand embroidered the numbers with a 1" wide fabric pole.

4. Complete with the barn road border accents.

Machine quilting along with a reverse buttonhole stitch echoes the straight lines to complete the barn.

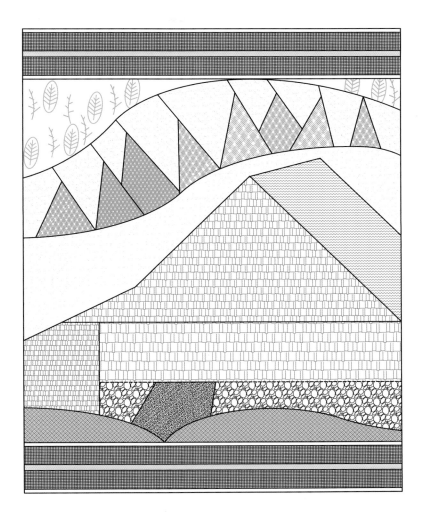

See the Patterns & Templates section for more.

Moon Over Mount Eagle Quilt

35½" × 28½"

Being a fan of Charlie Harper's graphics, I pay homage to his designs with my eagle rendering. My research proves there is a Mount Eagle in just about every state. You might also see a hint of our classic Moon Over the Mountain block. This wall hanging was our class project at the Nine Quarter Circle Ranch in 2009.

A sister to this quilt is part of a traveling exhibit assembled by Sue Wildemuth titled *Eagle Motifs in America: Decade Art Quilt Series 1770 to the Present*, with a companion book. Representations of historical eagle motifs from the 1770s to today from across the United States are presented by contemporary quilters telling the story of the American bald eagle, as the symbol of the United States, through 28 quilted wall hangings.

Method:

1. Cut a 21" × 29½" freezer paper/Grid Grip paper. Draw diagonal lines corner to corner. With a compass, draw a 4½" circle from the center point. Draw a 12¾" straight line on the circle top, parallel to the top line. Indicate the wings by connecting the corners up to that straight line.

2. Draw back tail under circle per directions. Code templates, noting mirror images of wing triangles in order to cut out in duplicate. Cut out all templates including the appliqué figures of A (the head), B (the beak), C (the eyes), and D (the triangle). Piece the tail templates to be joined with the side triangles that have a partial curve.

3. Connect the beak B to the head A and appliqué the eyes to the head. Appliqué this A, B, C figure to the sky. Stitch the side triangles to this sky, either by hand appliqué adding ¼" seam allowance, or by machine appliqué. Connect the curved moon to each of the triangles by pinning each end and center area. Remove paper for stitching, as it will not bend at the machine. Finish by sewing adjacent triangles together and then one diagonal line for the completed rectangle.

4. Side quarter-square triangles: cut four dark/light 4¼" squares; cut four light/other light 4¼" squares. Make quarter-square triangles with each combination to yield 16 squares that are 3½". You need only 14, so save the others for future projects. Sew seven blocks for each side border and attach to the rectangle.

5. The top band with the title was embroidered on my Bernina, cutting a 4" × 29" band. Trim to 3½" × 36".

6. The bottom band with feet and claws: cut two outside rectangles 3½" × 5"; cut two rectangles 5" × 12¼". For the claw rectangle: cut one dark square 4¼" and cut apart on each diagonal = four triangles. Cut four light squares 2⅜"; cut on the diagonal = eight triangles. Use the D template to cut four dark, three light, and two light half Ds.

Hand quilting completed this wall hanging.

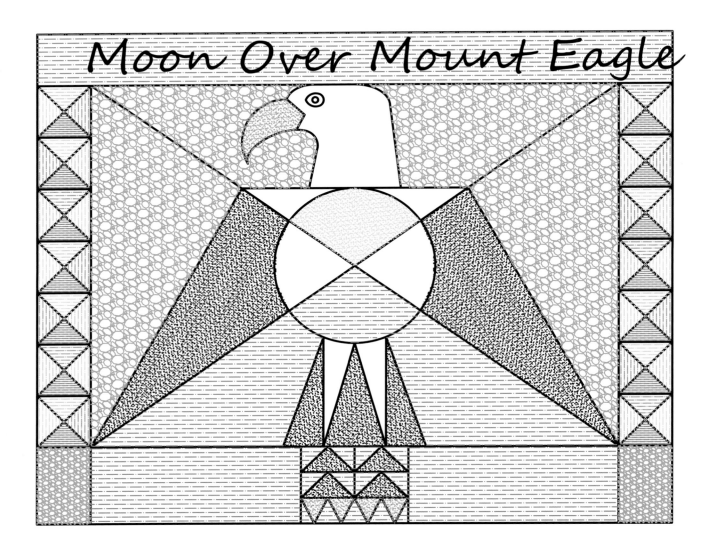

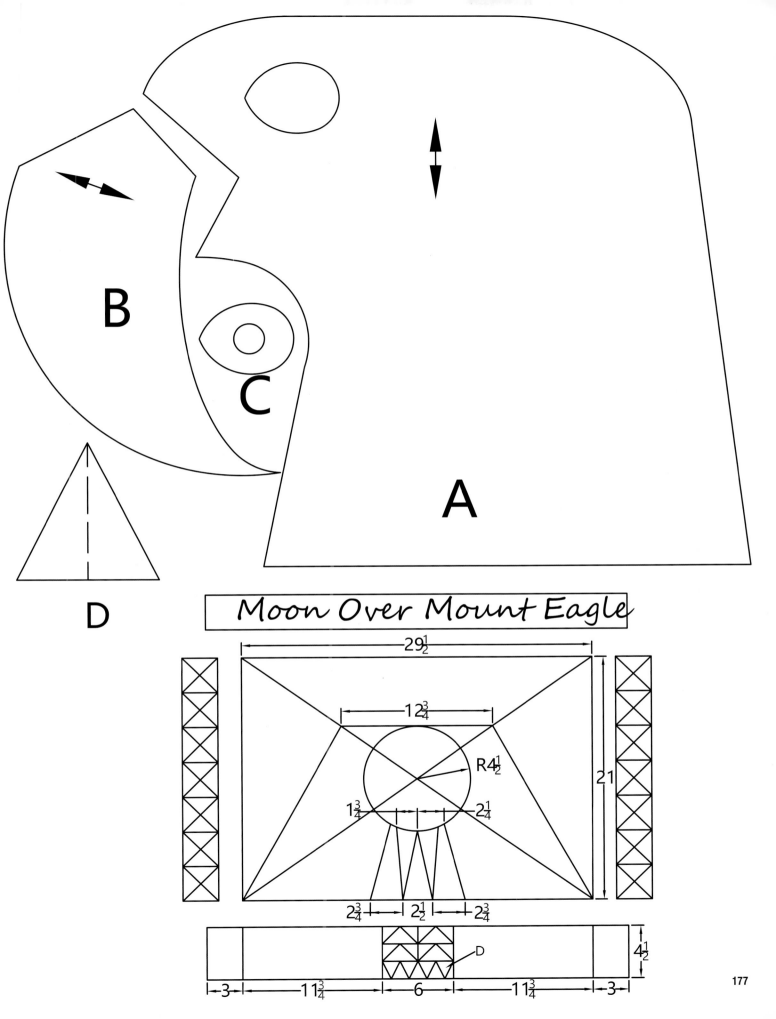

B

C

A

D

Moon Over Mount Eagle

$29\frac{1}{2}$

$12\frac{3}{4}$

R$4\frac{1}{2}$

21

$1\frac{3}{4}$ $2\frac{1}{4}$

$2\frac{3}{4}$ $2\frac{1}{2}$ $2\frac{3}{4}$

D

$4\frac{1}{2}$

3 $11\frac{3}{4}$ 6 $11\frac{3}{4}$ 3

Add a Bunny Quilt

19" × 38½"

Imagine more bunnies than Appaloosa horses at the Nine Quarter Circle Ranch in Montana (www.ninequartercircle .com). So, naturally, bunnies became the class project in 1996. This design is based on one of my favorite techniques: strip picture piecing. A few soft curves enhance the bunny head but mostly it is straight line stitching.

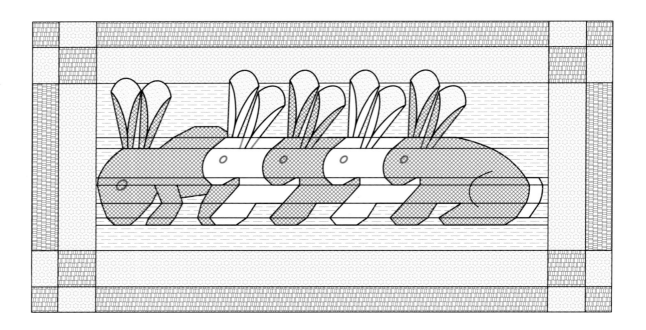

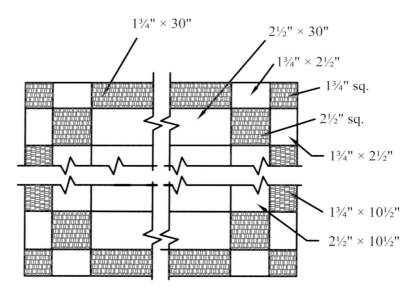

1¾" × 30"

2½" × 30"

1¾" × 2½"

1¾" sq.

2½" sq.

1¾" × 2½"

1¾" × 10½"

2½" × 10½"

Border dimensions.

**See the Patterns &
Templates section
for more.**

Fabric Requirements and Cutting:

Fat quarter of a variety of five rabbit fabric and pink ear fabric.

½ yard of grass background fabric.

Border cuts given below.

1. Transfer three pages of rabbits onto Grid Grip or freezer paper cut to 8½" × 11" on your home printer. Trim one template edge up to the line and press onto the next page for one continuous pattern. Identify the five rabbits with colored pencils or by naming the fabric. Cut apart each long row, keeping it intact until actual piecework begins.

2. Start with the A row. Cut apart each template on the piecing line, press onto the right side of fabric, add ¼" seam allowance on all sides, align paper edges by peeking under seam allowance, pin in place, and piece together. Grid Grip can be pressed onto the backside, add seam allowances, cut out with rotary cutter, and piece together following the edge of the paper. However, this does reverse the image. Do not stitch on the paper, as it can be peeled off and reused many times. Save and label templates for future projects. Hint: Measure the width of each row and cut fabric ½" wider so only two sides need to be trimmed. On the C row there are six curved areas. Use the Grid Grip for trimming seam allowances and pinning in place, but remove for stitching.

3. Ears: Press ear template on the backside of four layers pink/rabbit fabric to make two sets for each of the five rabbits. Sew around the oval edge of each set of ears; trim, invert, and press. Hand whipstitch the short ends together about 2". Insert ears between A, B, and C rows. Hand-tack ears in place to keep them from flopping.

4. Once all rows, A through G, are pieced with ears in place, add a bottom and top grass fabric to match the rabbit background: Cut 3" × 30½" for top border and cut 1¾" × 30½" for the bottom border.

Contrasting outside borders set off this wall hanging.

Sew two bands of light (cut 3" × 30½") and dark (cut 2¼" × 30½") fabric together and attach to the top and bottom of the rabbit rectangle.

Sew another two bands the same width only 11" long and attach four patches at each end, then sew on either side. The four patch cutting dimensions are:

Cut four dark 3" and 2¼" squares; and cut eight light rectangles 2¼" × 3". Following schematic, piece these together for corner four patches.

Hand quilting sets off each bunny, while a curved feather design on the machine highlights the border. Eyes or mouth addition is your choice.

Hint: As in any Grid Grip or freezer paper project the stability of a pressed template allows other fabric to be stacked underneath, cutting out more fabric.

Once the initial design is made, re-press the template on the waiting already-cut fabric.

Pipeline, Parkway, and Paul wall hanging. 35" × 50". It
pleases me to share another of my strip picture-piecing
efforts that was a challenge from the PTA quilt "groupies."
Due to an abundance of pink and green piping from some
factory, we were each given several yards and had to
create a wall hanging with the letter "P" as the inspiration.

Yard by yard life is hard, but inch

by inch it's a cinch!

—GB

The rooster may crow, but it's the hen that delivers the goods.

—Margaret Thatcher

Quilt Built

Warm the Walls with Fabric

I had seen fabric walls in magazines and even stayed in a bedroom in Paris where toile fabric continued from the walls up across the ceiling. Our "Quilt Built" home just had to have fabric on the walls somewhere. The dining room was perfect with its beadboard white wall halfway and continuous molding, which I painted yellow. But the figuring of how much toile fabric to buy was the challenge. Maybe this formula will help with your proposed project:

1. Measure the area to be covered; width times the height. Take into account the fabric repeat, which is often about 18" to be added for each height. Divide that by the width of the chosen fabric, eliminating the selvage. (in my case it was about 59 yards).

2. Two layers of batting were cut to size and stapled on the area to be covered. Start about 1" above the molding and extend upward to about an inch below the ceiling. This creates a soft texture to the area so the fabric extends outward a little.

3. Cut the fabric lengths and piece together, matching the prints. I pressed the seams open for a flat appearance. Then cut bias strips of the matching fabric 2" wide times the width for the base area and also the top ceiling area. Using a zipper foot, sew a covered tube inside the bias.

4. Sew this covered tube to the right side of the fabric for the entire width around the molding area. Also, at the very beginning, sew on a vertical tube that goes up to the ceiling. Now, let the fabric hang down and staple this around the molding area (backside showing). It is basically a staple-and-flip method. Once it is all stapled, bring the fabric upward, right sides showing, to tack temporarily at the top.

5. For the final top coverage, with a sturdy step ladder, use a hot glue gun to lightly secure the covered bias to the top of the wall, close to the ceiling.

My final tip is for the inside corners, of which there were four: It really helped for batting to not go all the way inside each indention so the staple gun could actually reach the fabric to be secured vertically at random, about every 18". Another set of hands helps toward the end for holding fabric in place: I called on my mother!

Blue Chairs No Longer

Think twice before painting chairs with two coats of blue paint. Little did I realize that these chairs were the first furniture my parents ever bought, in about 1934 in Primghar, Iowa. During my early "nesting" period, when it was all about decorating, I was given these chairs. Painting them blue was a necessity.

Fast forward over 50 years. As they were beat up, chipped, and outdated, I yearned for that original maple patina. So with lots of willpower, scraping, paint remover, and several sets of gloves, I got them back. To remind the family of their nostalgic meaning, they are now dated on the seat underside.

Before.

After.

My Maze

Having an outdoor walking maze is a special treat. No, I do not walk it every day and I do seem to spend more time pruning things, straightening rocks, and picking up debris, but it is such a soulful thing to have outside.

The beginning: setting the rocks on the weed-proof template with my granddaughter's help. Mulch covers in between the rocks.

The completed maze. Beware . . . what was once a little
plant may eventually flourish into a rhododendron bush.

Life is short, art is long.

—Hippocrates

CONCLUSION

Thank you for reading *Scrap Happy Quilts*. My hope is that you will be inspired to make many quilts for your home, family, and charity, and as gifts. I also hope my stories will motivate you to enter our fiber art field of quilt making. Not only to enjoy the work and camaraderie, but to become, maybe, a professional in a sewing-machine industry, or an authority on fiber research, or even a director of a major symposium. Explore all possibilities. I am proud to mention that the College of Textiles at North Carolina State University is where creativity and science meet, shaping global leaders in textile education research and service. We need the next generation of people to carry on this exciting field in their rightful place in time.

A heartfelt thank you to family and friends as they lived through this creative process with the author.

SCRAP HAPPY QUILTS' MAKERS AND QUILTERS

The Real Trip Around the World, Large: Georgia Bonesteel; longarm quilted by Sharis Myers. Medium and small: Georgia Bonesteel.

Scrap Soup, Large: Georgia Bonesteel; longarm quilted by Nancy Clayburn. Medium and Doll Bed Size: Georgia Bonesteel.

Cane Cousin: Georgia Bonesteel.

Lone Star (Large, Round table skirt, Wall hanging): Georgia Bonesteel.

Diamond Dazzle: Georgia Bonesteel.

Job's Troubles: pieced by Charlotte Bradshaw Sayler; hand quilted by Georgia Bonesteel.

Hummingbird Quilt: pieced by Ellen Kleffe Perkins; quilted by Penelope Ratzlaff Wortman.

Hall of Fame Autograph Quilt (Pillow shams): blocks signed and donated by many supporters of the Hall of Fame; designed and assembled by Georgia Bonesteel; quilted by Kathy Boxell.

Splashes: Georgia Bonesteel; longarm quilted by Debbie Beaver.

Log Cabin, Revisited with Denim: Georgia Bonesteel.

Sunflowers à la Marie Webster: pieced, appliquéd, and quilted by Georgia Bonesteel.

Not Everyone Likes Sunflowers wall hanging: Lorraine Rossi Tritthardt, longarm quilted by Anne Splotta.

Teapot Quilt: designed by Georgia Bonesteel; pieced by Lynda Carver, Betty Boyer, Sandy McGrady, Delta Peterson, Jo Seagle, Delores Southard, and Susan Worrell; longarm quilted by Dixie Stoltz.

Waste Not Want Not: Audrey Tews.

Roots: designed and appliquéd by Georgia Bonesteel and Linda Cantrell.

Comedy and Tragedy: Georgia Bonesteel.

Star Barn: Georgia Bonesteel.

Barn Storming with Tractor: Georgia Bonesteel.

Gray Barn with Red Roof: Georgia Bonesteel.

View from Below: Georgia Bonesteel.

Moon Over Mt. Eagle: Georgia Bonesteel.

Add a Bunny: Georgia Bonesteel.

PATTERNS & TEMPLATES

Lottie's Quilt (Job's Troubles)

Suggested quilting lines for Template B.

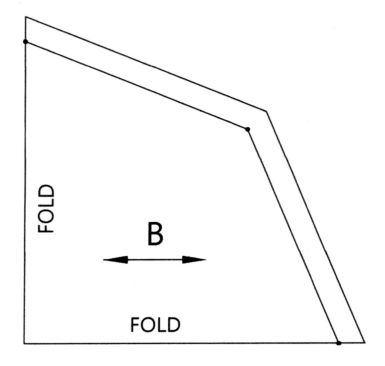

FOLD

FOLD

B

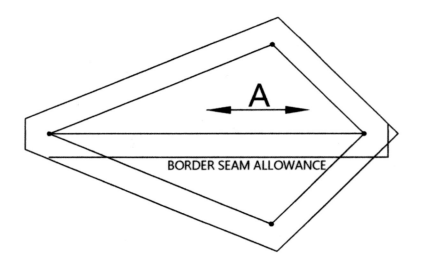

A

BORDER SEAM ALLOWANCE

Hummingbird Quilt

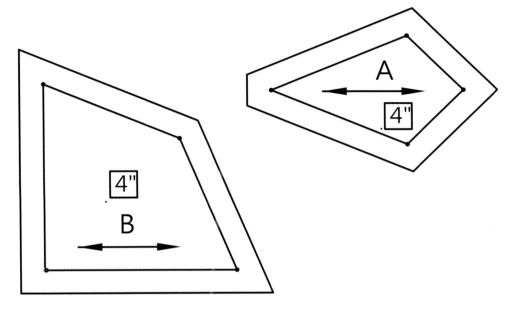

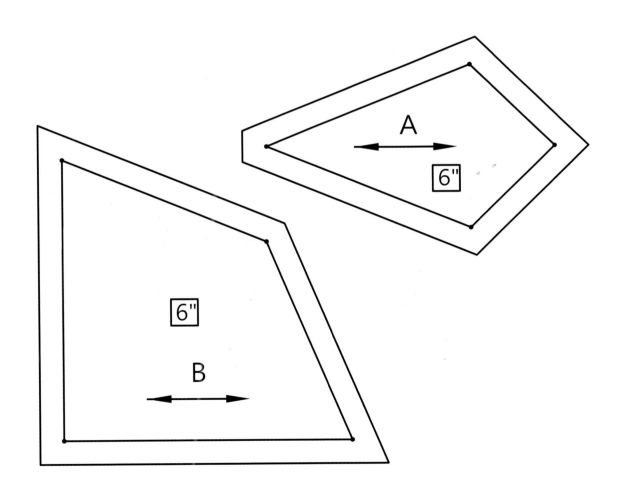

You may wonder about the irregularities of this quilting line pattern, but never fear. This is exactly how it is drawn and quilted, whether you make the smaller or larger version of the blocks.

Suggested quilting lines for the 4" blocks, Hummingbird Quilt background areas.

Suggested quilting lines for the 6" blocks, Hummingbird Quilt background areas.

Squares & Rectangles: Scrap Soup Quilt

Medium Scrap Soup

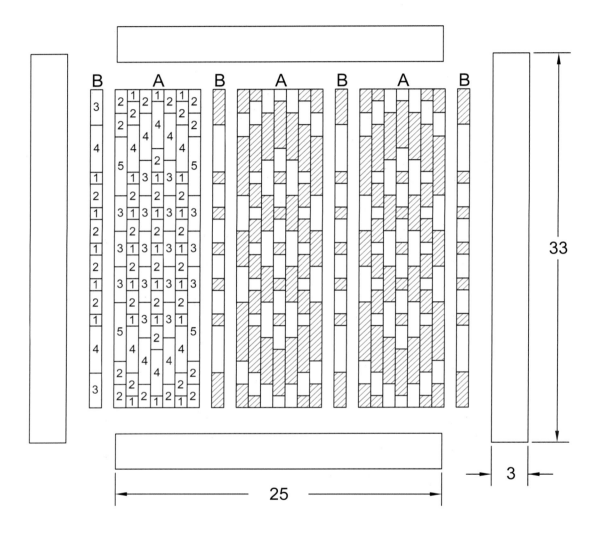

Miniature Scrap Soup

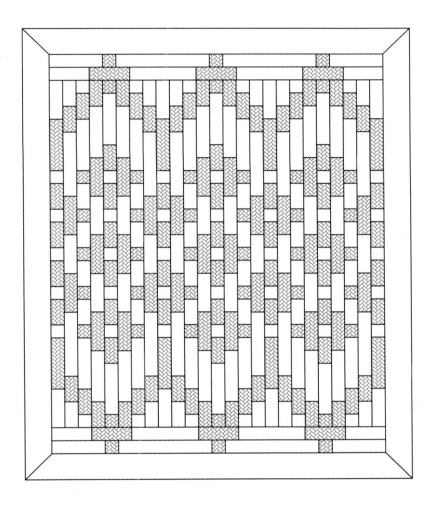

Triangles: Hall of Fame Autograph Quilt

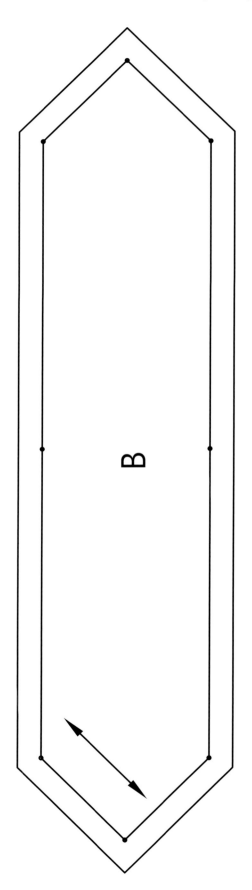

B

Equilateral Triangles: Cane Cousin Quilt

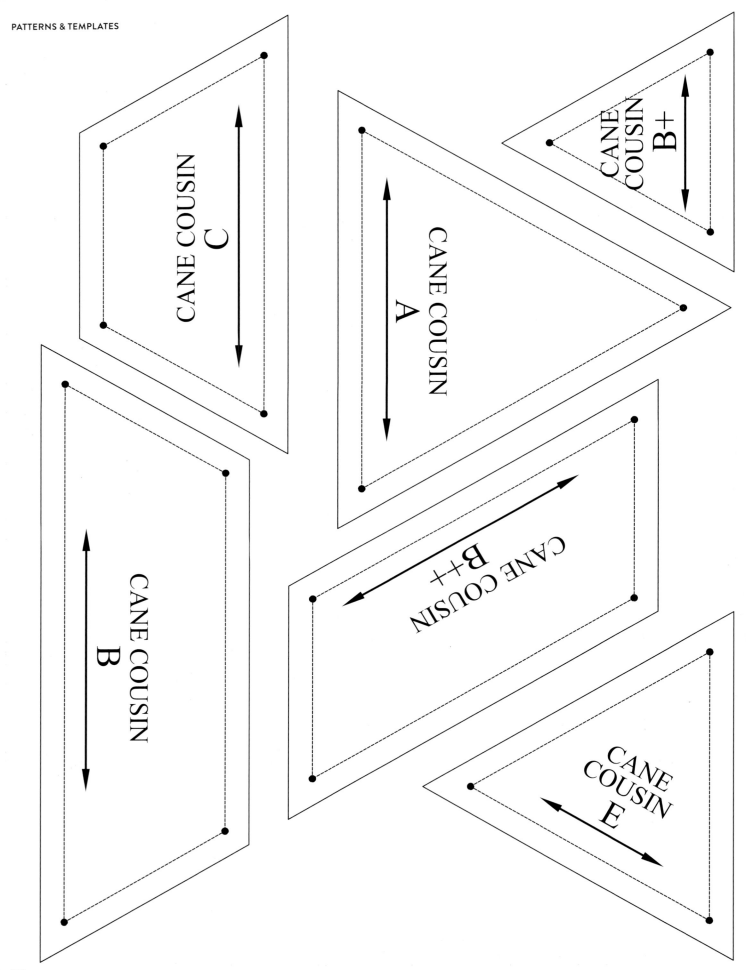

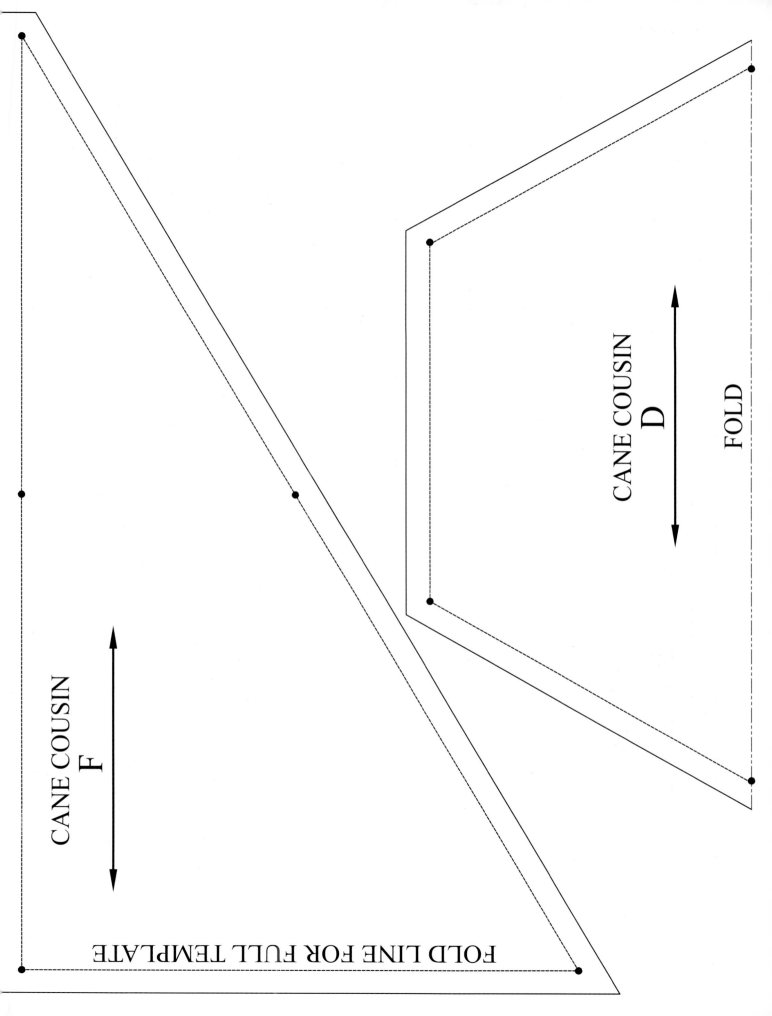

CANE COUSIN
F

FOLD LINE FOR FULL TEMPLATE

CANE COUSIN
D

FOLD

Sunflowers à la Marie Webster Quilt

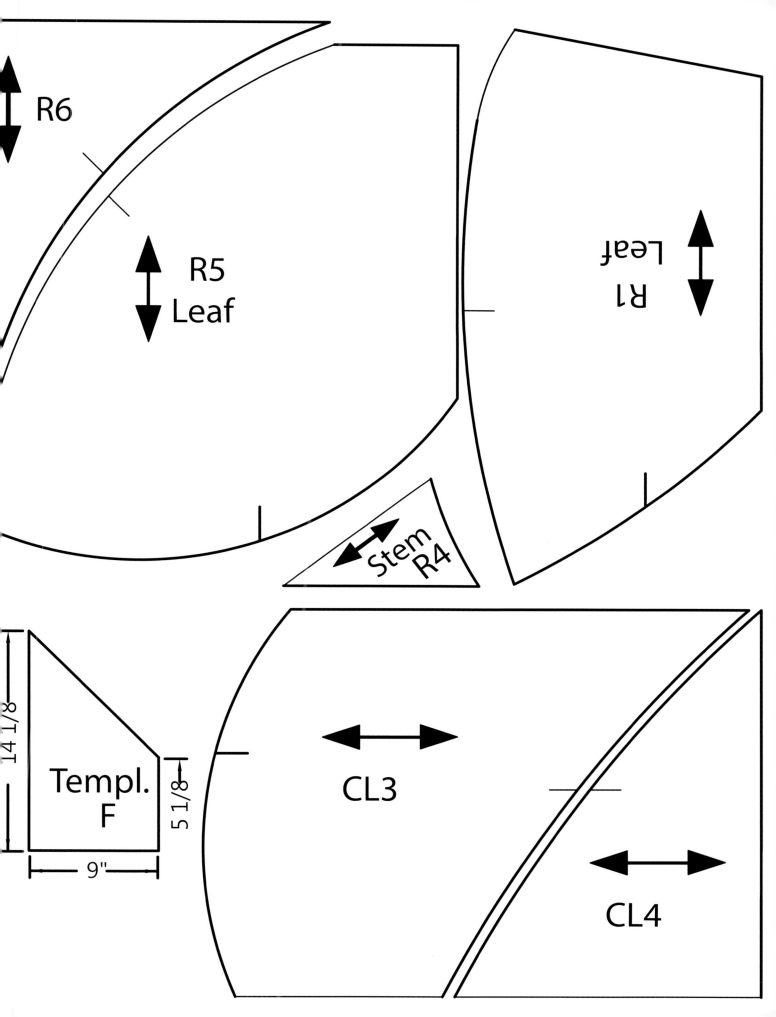

R6

R5
Leaf

R1
Leaf

Stem
R4

Templ.
F

14 1/8

5 1/8

9"

CL3

CL4

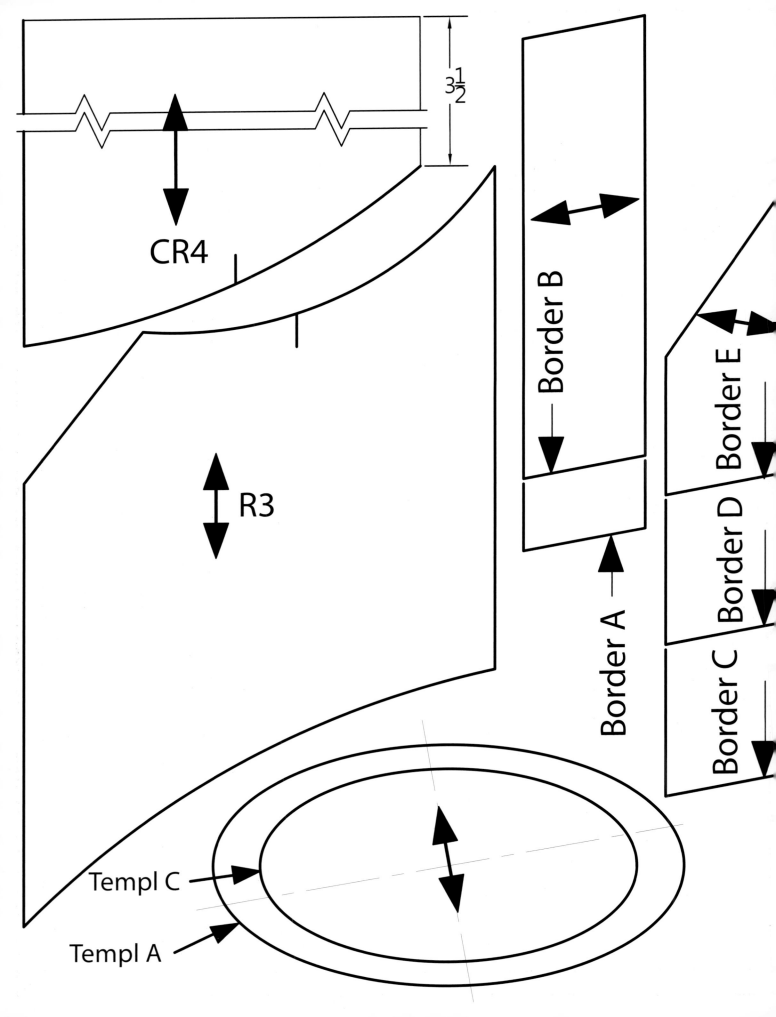

CR4

$3\frac{1}{2}$

R3

Border B

Border A

Border E

Border D

Border C

Templ C

Templ A

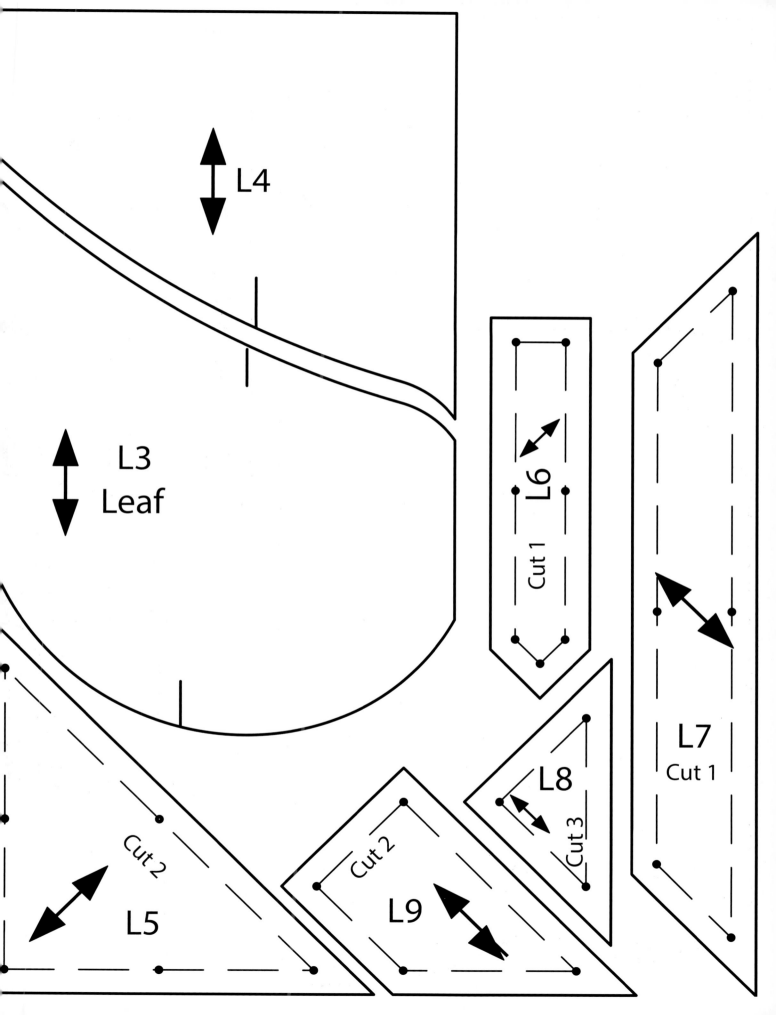

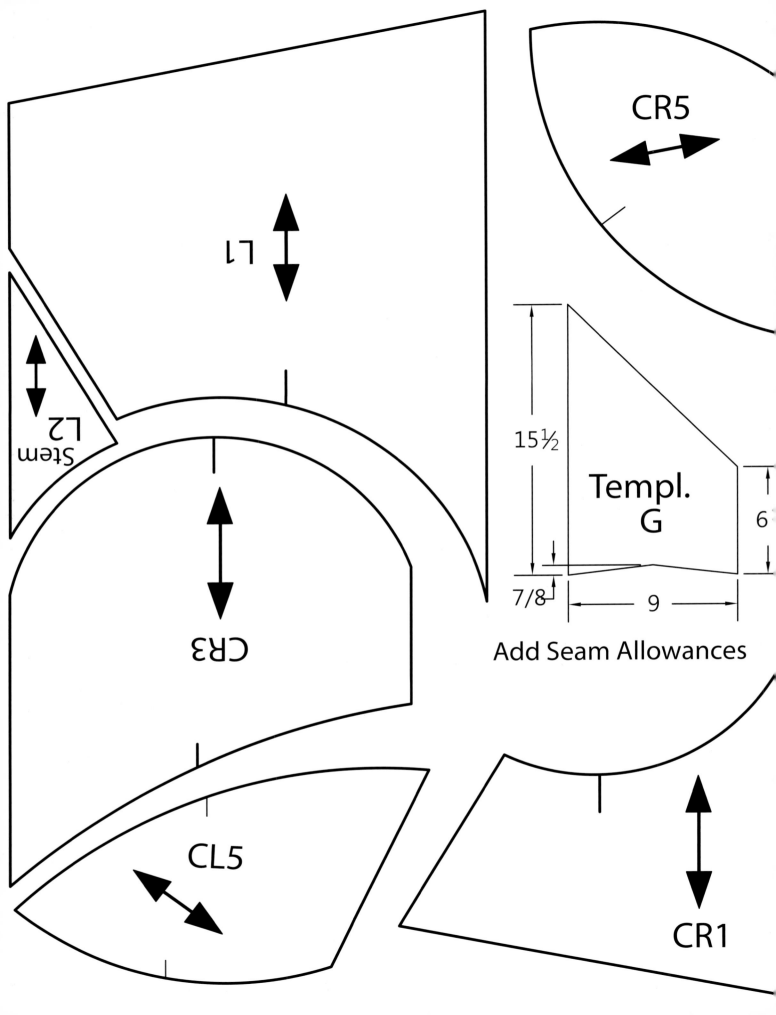

CR5

L1

L2
Stem

CR3

CL5

Templ.
G

15½

7/8

6

9

Add Seam Allowances

CR1

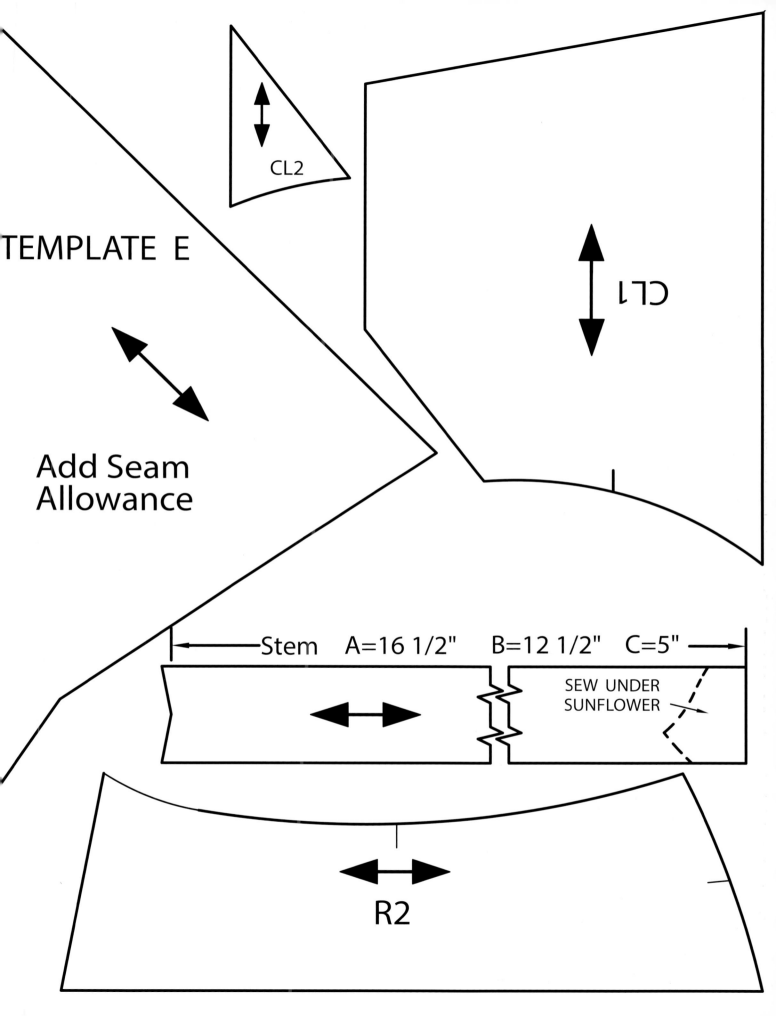

TEMPLATE E

CL2

CL1

Add Seam
Allowance

Stem   A=16 1/2"   B=12 1/2"   C=5"

SEW UNDER
SUNFLOWER

R2

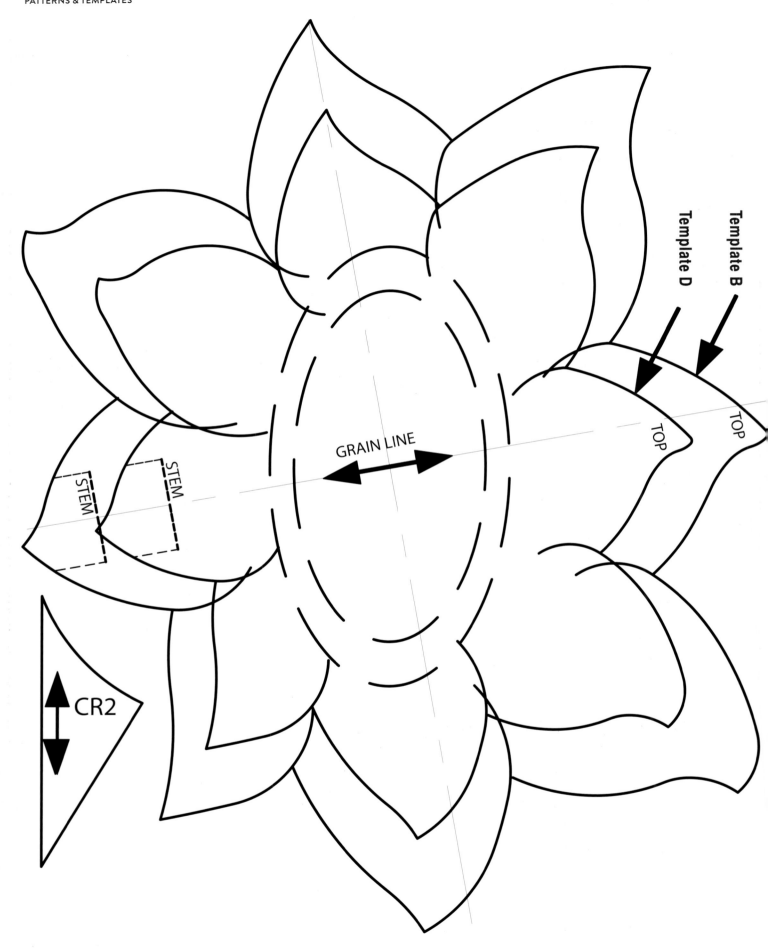

GRAIN LINE

STEM

STEM

CR2

Template B

Template D

TOP

TOP

The Teapot Quilt

This is a 10" block. Add ¼" seam allowance on all sides of templates.

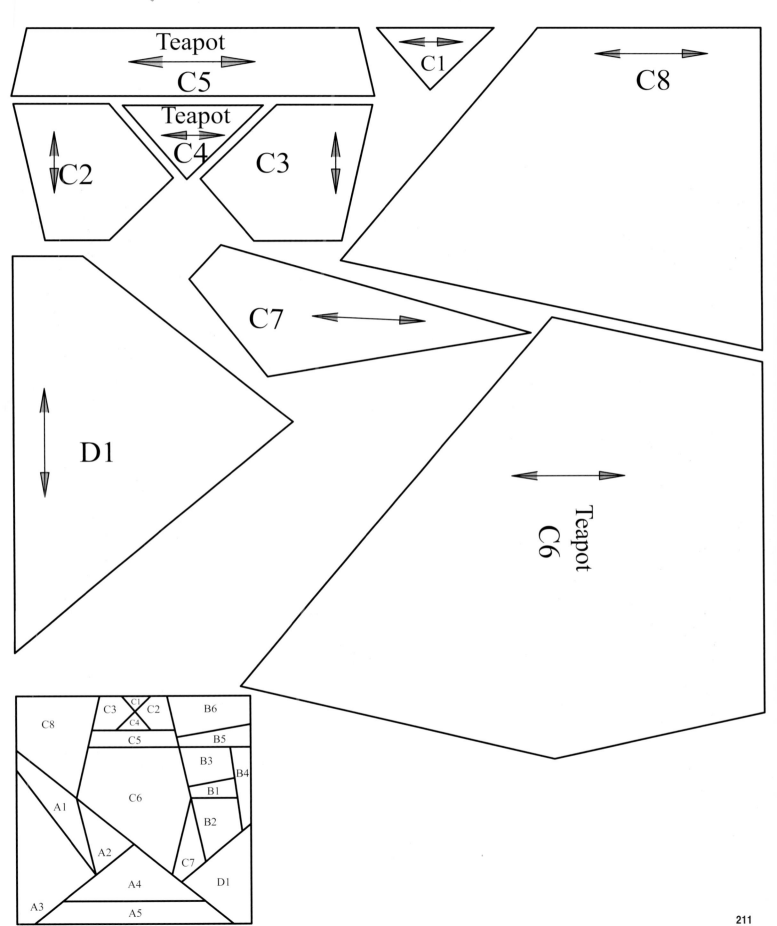

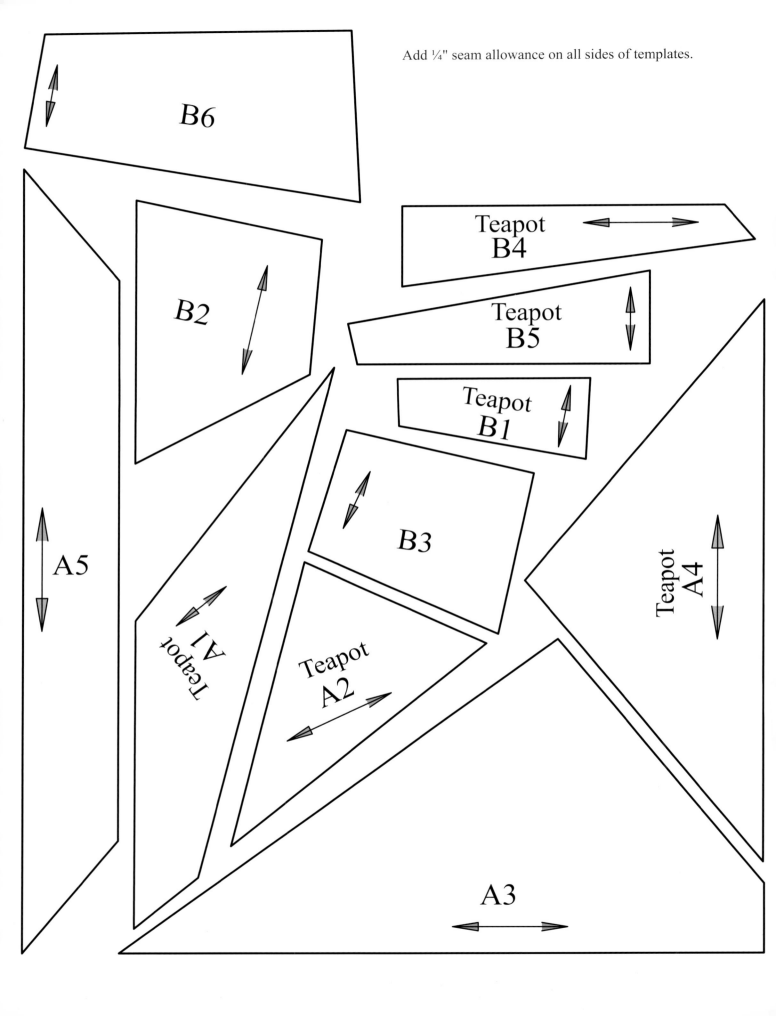

Comedy/Tragedy Quilt

This is a 14" block.

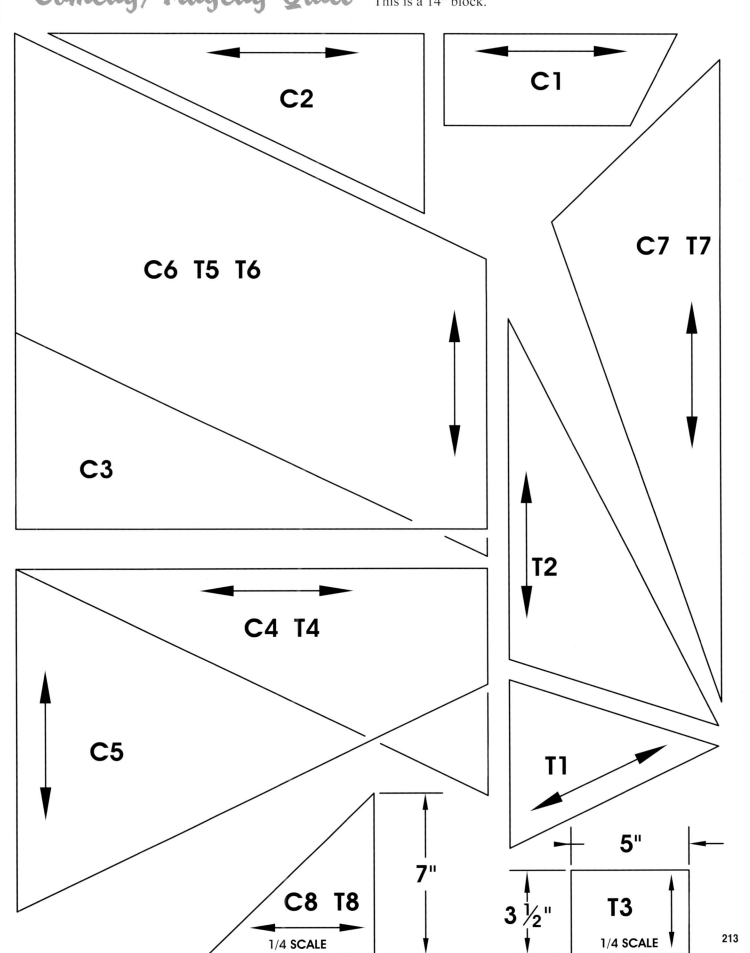

C1

C2

C6 T5 T6

C3

C7 T7

T2

C4 T4

C5

T1

7"

C8 T8

1/4 SCALE

5"

3 ½"

T3

1/4 SCALE

Star Barn

View from Below

Add ¼" seam allowance around each of these templates. Twinkle Toes slanted block. Piecing sequence marked starting at 1, etc.

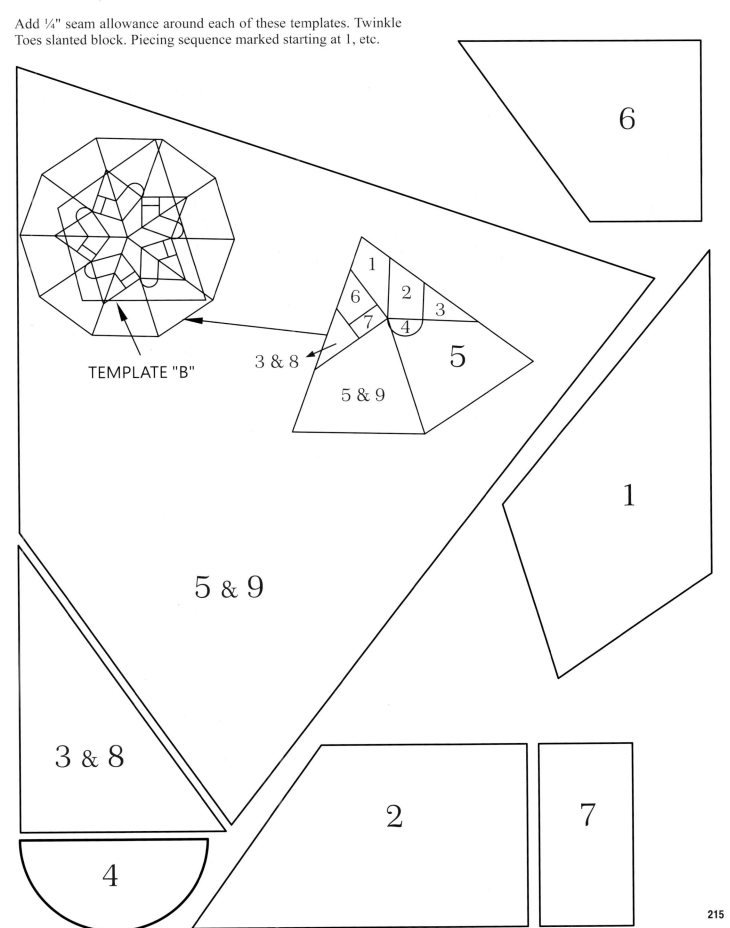

TEMPLATE "B"

3 & 8

5 & 9

6

1

5

5 & 9

3 & 8

2

7

4

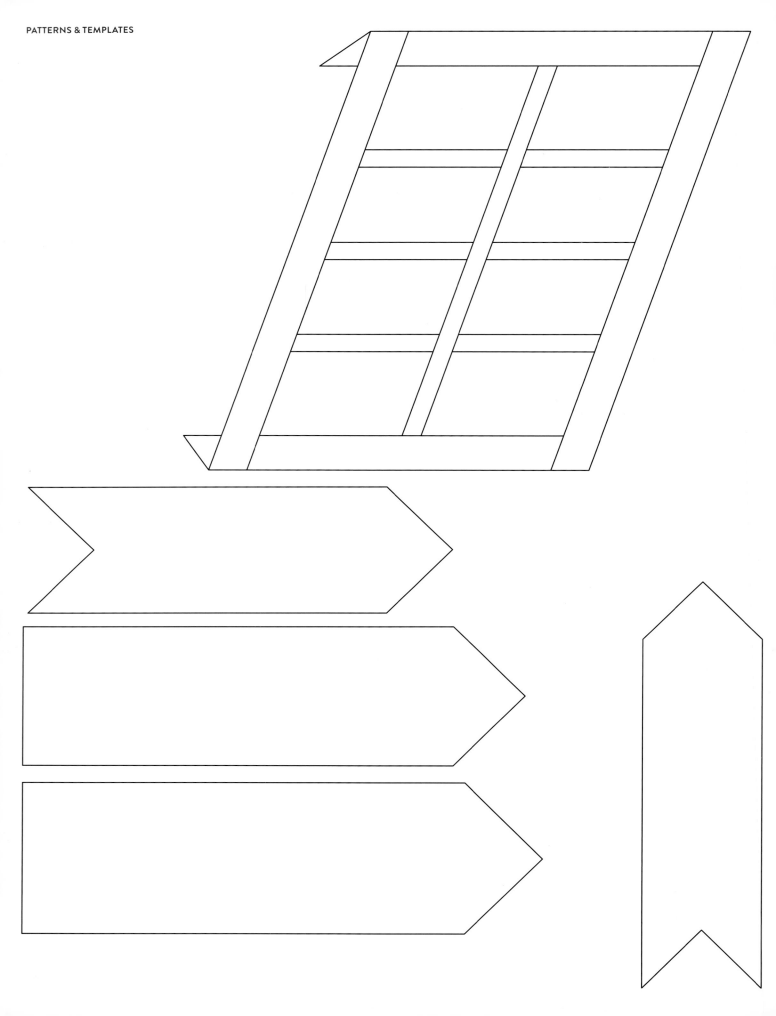

Barn with Tractor

Add ¼" seam allowance around each of these templates.

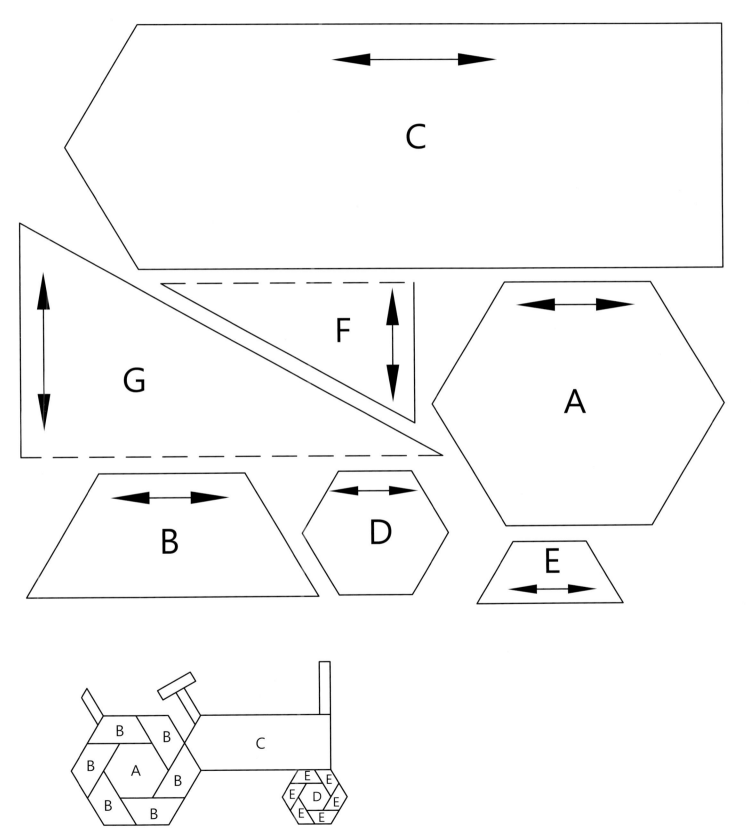

Gray Barn with Red Roof

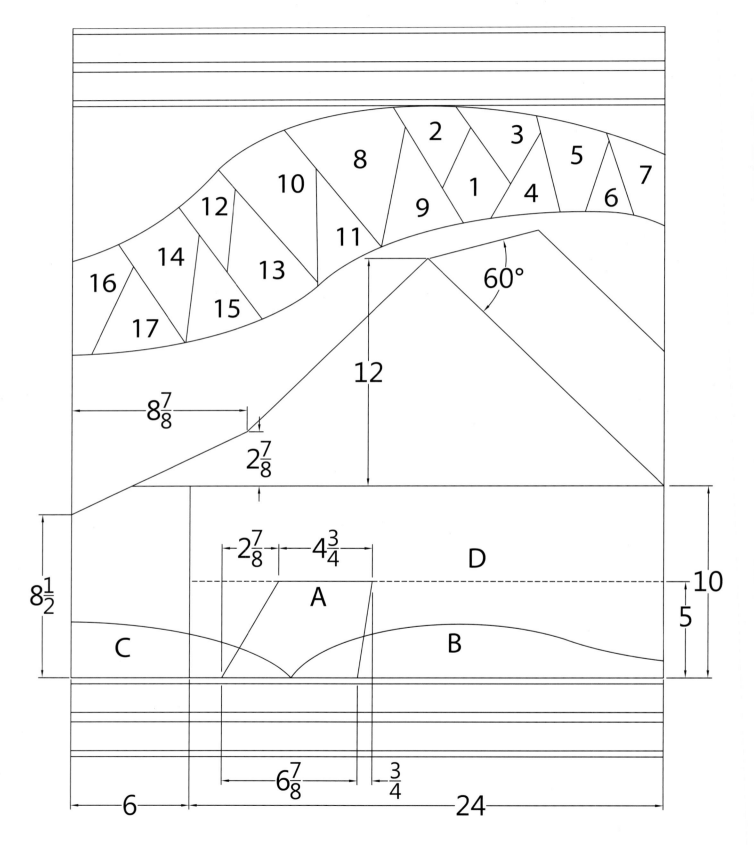